SANDWICH

Edible

Series Editor: Andrew F. Smith

EDIBLE is a revolutionary new series of books dedicated to food and drink that explores the rich history of cuisine. Each book reveals the global history and culture of one type of food or beverage.

Already published

Sandwich

A Global History

Bee Wilson

REAKTION BOOKS

To my father, who makes a fine tomato sandwich.

Published by Reaktion Books Ltd
33 Great Sutton Street
London EC1V 0DX, UK
www.reaktionbooks.co.uk

First published 2010

Printed and bound in China

British Library Cataloguing in Publication Data

Wilson, Bee.
Sandwich : a global history. – (Edible)
1. Sandwiches. 2. Sandwiches – History.
1. Title 11. Series
641.8´4-DC22

ISBN: 978 1 86189 771 8

Contents

Introduction

At last! No more cooking. I can eat what I really like – sandwiches!

A widow in the 1970s, quoted in David Kynaston, *Family Britain 1951–1957* (London, 2009)

Portable, quick, satisfying, cheap and requiring neither plate nor cutlery, the sandwich is the most universal of all fast food, the archetypal hand-held snack. With the exception of people who don't eat bread, for whatever reason, all of us eat sandwiches – and in an unusually wide range of contexts. They are eaten by school children and High Court judges, by soldiers and pacifists, by busy call-centre workers and leisurely picnickers. They are eaten in hospital wards, in prisons, in the lounges of four-star hotels and at the kitchen table. The sandwich is simply the quickest way of making a meal. We may speak and dream of other foods; we may pontificate on banquets and gastronomy; but a lot of the time, if we are honest, what we are really eating is sandwiches.

'Sandwiches in the twenty-first century,' writes the food historian Andrew F. Smith, 'are consumed in some form in almost every country in the world.'[1] In 1986 Irena Chalmers and Milton Glaser estimated that Americans eat 45 billion sandwiches a year, which works out at around 193 sandwiches

Pop-Art sandwiches (used to market 'SoHo Sandwiches', a New York-themed sandwich company based in North London).

A sandwich menu, United States.

per person. A more recent estimate, according to Smith, ups that number to 198 sandwiches per head (as against 100 hamburgers). In the UK, similarly, it is estimated that two hundred sandwiches per person are consumed every year – in other words, we eat sandwiches on more days of the year than not. Definitive figures are hard to come by, however, because unlike pizza or hamburgers or fried chicken, sandwiches are made at home at least as often as they are bought. The UK commercial sandwich market is worth around £3.5 billion (as against £1 billion for commercial pizza). In addition, the British Sandwich Association estimates that £3.86 billion is spent every year by British consumers on 'lunchboxes that contain 2.67 billion sandwiches, and a further 6.24 billion sandwiches are made at home'.[2] After that, it's guesswork. No one knows how many sandwiches are made and consumed worldwide, but the number must be colossal.

What makes the sandwich so appealing? It is deeply convenient, infinitely variable, cheap and filling. It can be eaten anywhere, with as much or as little ceremony as you like. All you need is a hearty appetite and a single hand – the other remains free to read a book, flick the TV remote, hold a phone, pick your nose, gesticulate in conversation or check emails. The sandwich represents liberation from the constraints and rules of formal meals; and for that reason, it has attracted enemies as well as friends. Ever since the fourth Earl of Sandwich first gave his name to a piece of meat inside two slices of bread, some have viewed it as a threat to sociability and to all the nourishing properties of a good, hot meal.

Sandwiches take so many different forms that it is hard to find a definition to fit them all. A sandwich can be a hearty doorstop or a fragile triangle of paper-thin cucumber on slender white bread; it can be a piping-hot Indian toasted sandwich of potato curry and chutney or a fridge-cold pre-packed tuna mayo 'wedge'; it can be a Vietnamese vegetarian hoagie of tofu and pickles or a towering American deli sandwich in which the mammoth layer of cured meats and cheese dwarfs the thickness of the bread. In short, the sandwich is a dish in which bread is used as a vehicle for some kind of filling – maybe meat, but just as easily almost anything else. The best-selling Victorian cookery writer Mrs Beeton even gives a recipe for a toast sandwich, in which buttered bread is filled with toasted bread – good for invalids, apparently.[3]

The *OED* definition of a sandwich is rather a mouthful:

> An article of food for a light meal or snack, composed of two thin slices of bread, usually buttered, with a savoury (originally specifying meat, especially beef or ham) or other filling. Frequently with specifying word prefixed indicating contents, as ham, egg, watercress, peanut butter sandwich or form, as club, Dagwood, Denver, hero, poor boy, submarine sandwich. Occasionally with only one slice of

bread, as in open or open-faced sandwich, or with biscuits, sliced buns or cake.

This is both too narrow and too broad. It is too prescriptive to say that a sandwich is composed of 'two thin slices of bread' (what of the chip butty or the bacon bap?). On the other hand, it is too broad to allow in the definition sandwiches made with 'only one slice of bread'. Although a delicious component of many cuisines in Scandinavia, Russia and the Balkans, the open sandwich should never really have been given the name. Structurally, the open sandwich is a contradiction in terms. Open sandwiches are fine things, but not sandwiches.

The versatility of sandwiches: a couple sharing one in 1964.

Scandinavian 'open sandwiches': very delicious but not true sandwiches.

A true sandwich necessarily carries with it the idea of enclosure. It consists of bread surrounding a filling (even when that filling is simply more bread, à la Mrs Beeton). The containment may be achieved through various different means – whether the soft folding layers of a wrap, the crusty hinged opening of a sliced-open roll or the classic two-slice structure eaten by the fourth Earl of Sandwich in the eighteenth century. But there must be containment – a bready top as well as a bottom – if the term sandwich is to have a consistent meaning. Otherwise, you could say that plain buttered bread, or the French *tartine* is a sandwich; or beans on toast, scrambled eggs on toast or anything else on toast; or a *bruschetta* of tomato and basil. Logically, this is nonsense. However intricately and beautifully constructed, the Scandinavian 'open sandwich' or *smörgås* (foundation of the smörgasbőrd) is not a sandwich, because here the bread is topped rather than filled. You can add layers to a sandwich – double and triple deckers are still sandwiches. But the minimum is two slices of bread, or the equivalent formed from a roll or flatbread.

Many things have been called 'sandwiches' which are not. You can take two lettuce leaves, put a slice of cheese between

Afternoon tea sandwiches.

them and call it a 'slimmer's sandwich' but that still doesn't make it a sandwich, any more than a sandwich sponge cake, or a tower of grilled aubergine interlaced with slices of mozzarella, or an Oreo cookie are sandwiches, though all take their inspiration from the classical form of the true sandwich. In spring 2010 the KFC chain in America launched a supposed 'sandwich' (the 'Double Down') in which the bread is replaced with slabs of fried chicken filled with cheese, bacon and mayonnaise. It was 'so meaty, there's no room for a bun', claimed KFC. The *New York Times* restaurant critic deemed it 'a slimy and unnaturally moist thing'. The real outrage was that this greasy stack of meat should call itself a 'sandwich'.

All this may sound pedantic, but sometimes it matters. In 2006 a judge in Worcester, Massachusetts ruled that a Mexican burrito was not a sandwich. The Panera Bread Co. had been attempting to bar a rival firm, the Qdoba Mexican grill, from doing business in the White City shopping mall on the grounds that the chain's burritos violated an exclusivity agreement that only they (the Panera Bread Co.) were allowed to sell sandwiches in the mall. The judge, Jeffrey A. Locke, disagreed. He relied on the affidavit of local chef Chris Schlesinger who testified that 'I know of no chef or culinary historian who would call a burrito a sandwich.' The judge himself concluded that the critical point was the number of slices of bread, arguing: 'A sandwich is not commonly understood to include burritos, tacos, and quesadillas, which are typically made with a single tortilla and stuffed with a choice filling of meat, rice, and beans.'[4]

It was good of the judge to try to lay down the law here, but in the end his ruling was probably too narrow. We don't want to have to exclude from the sandwich family houmous and falafel pitta bread sandwiches, along with the host of 'wraps' that currently make up so much of the commercial sandwich market. This would be tricky, especially since there are grounds for arguing that the wrap – in the form of the Passover matzo-maror sandwich – is the oldest sandwich on record. It is certainly true, however, that some foods encased in bread, of which burritos are one, have taken on a life of their own which pushes them beyond the category of the sandwich. Hamburgers and hotdogs are technically sandwiches, but we will not consider them as such here. The sandwich is big enough as it is.

So is it possible to define the sandwich? A workable technical definition might be: two or more slices of bread, or the equivalent in rolls, flatbread or other baked goods, used as a structure to contain a filling of some other food, whether hot or cold, to make a meal, such that no utensils are necessary. But we must try not to get hung up on technicalities. Above all else, the sandwich is a way of life, one originally associated with a restless English earl in the eighteenth century.

I

The History of the Sandwich: The Fourth Earl and What Came Before

He freed mankind from the hot lunch. We owe him so much.

Funeral oration delivered to the Earl of Sandwich, as imagined
by Woody Allen in *Getting Even*, 1971

Viewed historically, the 'sandwich' is a riddle. Common sense tells us that the thing itself – meat, cheese or whatever else happened to be to hand wedged inside bread – must be one of the oldest and most universal types of meal, at least in bread-eating countries. Yet the name itself is very specific and belongs to one man – the fourth Earl of Sandwich, John Montagu (1718–1792), who, too busy to stop for dinner, called for some beef between two slices of bread. So the earl gets credited with inventing something that must have been around for hundreds if not thousands of years.

As a method of filling the belly, the sandwich is as basic and eternal as soup. As the *Larousse Gastronomique* notes, 'It has long been the custom in rural France, for example, to give farm labourers working in the fields meat for their meal enclosed in two slices of brown bread.'[1] The same was true

John Montagu, fourth Earl of Sandwich, painted by Thomas Gainsborough, 1783.

in all the peasant countries of Europe. Workers did not need to give this snack a name. It was just what you ate.

In an epigram circulating in Regency England about the Earl Spencer (who popularized a short jacket) and the Earl of Sandwich, 'the one invented half a coat/the other half a dinner'.[2] But it cannot be that John Montagu 'invented' the sandwich in the way that Auguste Escoffier invented Peach Melba, or Caesar Cardini invented the Caesar salad. The earl did not set out to be a culinary innovator, and he certainly was not the first person to eat the food that now bears his name.

A story by Woody Allen ('Yes, But Can the Steam Engine Do This?') plays with the absurdity of anyone inventing such a thing as the sandwich.[3] In the story, the Earl of Sandwich discovers as a child that he has 'an unusual interest in thinly sliced strips of roast beef and ham'. In his early fixation with

American migrant workers snatching a quick outdoor sandwich in 1959: meals such as this one must have taken place for hundreds of years before the official invention of the sandwich.

inventing the sandwich, he endures many disasters. His first attempt is two slices of bread topped with a slice of turkey. Then he tries three slices of ham all on top of one another, with no bread. Finally, in triumph, in the small hours of 27 April 1758, the earl thinks to place ham and mustard inside two slices of rye bread – eureka! His invention is instantly feted. There is clearly something comically absurd about giving the sandwich a single point of origin, as if it were a light bulb or a spinning jenny.

Nevertheless, it is striking how rapidly the 'sandwich' became established in the language in the space of just a few years in the 1760s and '70s, and how it has remained there, forever linked to John Montagu's name. While Montagu didn't invent the 'sandwich' per se, we cannot ignore the fact that every time we eat one, we invoke his name. Why?

The usual story, repeated in almost every potted history of the sandwich, is this: the earl was an inveterate gambler, who was so busy playing all-night cards that he was unwilling to leave the table to get something to eat. Being hungry, he ordered a piece of meat between two slices of bread to be brought to him at the card table. The source of this story is a chatty French travel book, Grosley's *Tour of London* (first published in 1770 as *Londres*), based on a stay in London during 1765. Grosley wrote:

> A minister of state passed four and twenty hours at a public gaming-table, so absorpt in play, that, during the whole time, he had no subsistence but a piece of beef, between two slices of toasted bread, which he eat without ever quitting the game. This new dish grew highly in vogue, during my residence in London: it was called by the name of the minister who invented it.[4]

A SANDWICH.

Pub Feb 8 1788 by S W Fores Satirist N 3 Piccadilly.

8 feb 1788

A man sandwiched by two women, hand-coloured etching, 1788: this image shows how rapidly the notion of 'sandwiching' took off.

The fourth earl's biographer, the naval historian N.A.M. Rodger, casts doubt on this account. In 1765 Montagu was a cabinet minister and 'very busy', with little time for all-night gambling sessions.[5]

In truth, Montagu's reputation as a notorious gambler was hardly justified. He was not averse to placing the odd wager – for example, he laid down fifty guineas that the Chevalier d'Eon, a transvestite French diplomat, was not a woman – and he enjoyed having small bets with his Huntingdonshire neighbours on the relative distances of various country roads. But by the standards of his contemporaries, his gambling was not excessive (not least because by the standards of the British aristocracy, he was poor).[6] The alternative explanation is that instead of being engrossed at the card table, Montagu was busily at work at his desk. He was a politician of tremendous, restless energy who twice served as First Lord of the Admiralty (in 1748–51 and again in 1771–83), once as Postmaster General (in 1768) and twice as Secretary of State (from 1763 and 1770). At the Admiralty, he was responsible for the vast job of reforming the entire British naval administration. Rodger finds the desk explanation plausible, since 'we have ample evidence of the long hours he worked from an early start, in an age when dinner was the only substantial meal of the day, and the fashionable hour to dine was four o'clock'.[7]

The sandwich is the ideal desk-bound meal for someone so immersed in paper that they have no time to stop. The crucial innovation of a sandwich, as opposed to a plate containing its component parts – bread and cheese or bread and meat – is that it can be eaten one-handed. The other hand is free to turn pages, sign documents, write letters – in other words, to carry on as if no food were being consumed at all. Orlando Montagu, who is the fourth earl's great-great-great-

great-great-great grandson, remarks that 'our family suffers from a patience deficit'.[8]

But as the word took hold as it did – by 1773, it was used in a cookbook for the first time[9] – there must sometimes have been witnesses to John Montagu's sandwich-eating, which suggests that he did not always eat them alone. And these witnesses must have found something distinctive enough in Montagu's sandwich habit that they thought to name it after him. A tall, awkward man with a fondness for skittles and a passion for music (his long-standing mistress, Martha Ray, was an opera singer), Sandwich clearly had the kind of character that made people want to name things after him. Captain Cook, who reported to him at the Admiralty, named the Sandwich Islands (now the Hawaiian Islands) after him. The naming of the sandwich suggests that people emulated him in more trivial matters too. Sandwich's friends must have seen him or heard him ordering his cold meat between two slices of bread and asked for 'the same as Sandwich' or words to that effect. Within a few months or years 'the same as Sandwich' was shortened to 'sandwich'.

The first known use of the word comes from another great man of the age. On 24 November 1762 the historian Edward Gibbon (author of *The Rise and Fall of the Roman Empire*) recorded in his *Journal* an evening spent in London. He dined with his friend Holt at the Cocoa-Tree in St James's Street, and then saw a production of Dryden's *The Spanysh Fryar*. He then returned to the Cocoa-Tree, of which he wrote:

> That respectable body, of which I have the honour to be a member, affords every evening a sight truly English. Twenty or thirty, perhaps, of the first men in the kingdom, in point of fashion and fortune, supping at little

Beef between two slices of bread: the original sandwich as eaten by the fourth Earl.

tables covered in a napkin, in the middle of a coffee-room, upon a bit of cold meat, or a Sandwich, & drinking a glass of punch.[10]

This tells us a great deal: that the early 'sandwich' was usually filled with cold meat, that it was eaten at the highest echelons of the British establishment and that it was considered a supper or post-theatre dish which might be eaten long after dinner.

Yet Gibbon leaves many questions unanswered, including the basic one of how the sandwich got its name. How widely was it known outside this circle of 'twenty or thirty' men at the Cocoa-Tree? And for how long before 1762 had the sandwich been known as the sandwich?

Given the date of Gibbon's diary entry, the likeliest time for the birth of Sandwich's sandwich is 1748–51, during his first stint as First Lord of the Admiralty. At that time, Montagu was a famous thirty-something about town, rushed off his feet at work and linked to London club life through his connections with the notorious Hellfire club. During the 1750s, he separated from his wife, who had been declared insane, and for a while retreated to a quieter life at his estate, Hinchingbrooke in Huntingdonshire, where he had access to his own home-reared beef and a fine kitchen garden. It is likely that he sometimes ate cold beef between two slices of bread here too but, if so, there were few outside his household to take notice. For the 'sandwich' to take off among Gibbon and his circle by 1762, it seems likely that it was ordered by the earl in the gossipy world of London.

We will probably never know for sure. The most interesting question in any case is not the first time that John Montagu ate cold beef between bread but the first time that someone else, copying him, ordered 'a sandwich'. They, and not he, were the inventor of the word in its current meaning. In the absence, however, of a hitherto unearthed contemporary chronicler recounting this moment, we are stuck with 1762 as the founding moment for the 'sandwich'.

Orlando Montagu, a young entrepreneur and son of the current earl, has done the obvious thing and gone into the sandwich business. In 2003, with the conveniently named

Robert Earl (the founder of Planet Hollywood and the Hard Rock Café), Montagu founded Earl of Sandwich, a chain of restaurants with venues in Walt Disney World in Florida and Detroit Airport among many others. Earl of Sandwich sells hot 'made-to-order' sandwiches – the meat is all roasted and the bread is all baked fresh on the premises – with a 'historical' theme. 'The sandwich you'd make if your name was on it' reads a legend emblazoned on the walls.[11] The menu includes the Full Montagu, the Earl's Club Sandwich and 'an original 1762', harking back to Gibbon, which consists of hot roast beef with a slice of cheese and strong horseradish on warm bread. Though he shares his ancestor's energy and drive, Orlando disagrees with him on the virtues of cold leftovers. 'I think cold is bad. Cold food just doesn't taste as good.'[12] With this new family brand of hot sandwiches, Montagu is optimistically trying to reclaim 'the sandwich with a capital "s"'.[13] As the company tagline says, 'The Original Sandwich since 1762'.

What, though, of sandwiches before 1762 – sandwiches *avant la lettre*? The earl cannot have been the first person who, wanting some cold meat and some bread, thought to place the one inside the other. Particularly in an era before the use of the fork, it would have been the neatest and most obvious way of eating bread and cheese or bread and meat without getting your fingers dirty. There is, however, a frustrating lack of evidence for sandwiches before 1762.

Some sources have suggested that the ancient Romans ate a kind of 'sandwich-like' snack called 'offula' or 'ofellae'.[14] These were certainly a kind of snack, and were eaten in taverns, but 'sandwich-like' is pushing it. *Ofulla* seems, rather, to have been an all-purpose term for snack, rather like 'tapas': sometimes they were morsels of marinated meat, sometimes starchy lumps of polenta; hardly a sandwich.

Another dead-end is the medieval trencher – large pieces of bread on which food was served. These have frequently been compared to sandwiches and one author of a book on sandwiches proposes that in the Middle Ages sandwiches 'were known as trenchers'.[15] It is undoubtedly true that, like sandwiches, trenchers were a form of bread used as a vehicle for eating other foods. There, however, the similarity ends. Unlike a sandwich, with a trencher, the meat and the bread were not eaten together. The trencher's role was primarily that of an edible plate. At rich feasts, trenchers would be removed several times during the meal and replaced with fresh ones.[16] The meat-soaked trencher would later be eaten by the servants. Eating someone else's juice-soaked hunk of bread is not the same as eating your own sandwich.

A more plausible – and much older – candidate for the first sandwich is the *Korech* or 'Hillel sandwich', eaten as part of the Jewish Passover meal. In the first century BC Hillel the Elder (born *circa* 110 BC), a distinguished rabbi, created the custom of eating bitter herbs sandwiched together inside matzo bread, the herbs (*maror*) symbolizing the bitterness of slavery and the unleavened bread commemorating the hasty flatbreads made by the Israelites as they fled Egypt. In the Bible, Exodus 12:8, the rules of Passover state that 'they shall eat the flesh in that night, roast with fire, and unleavened bread; and with bitter herbs they shall eat it'. According to the *Haggadah*, the Jewish religious text setting out the rules for the Seder meal, Hillel took the prescriptions of Exodus and Numbers and turned them into a living ritual. 'This is what Hillel did when the Temple existed: He enwrapped the Paschal lamb, the matzo and the bitter herbs to eat them as one.' In other words, he made a lamb-and-herb sandwich.

The matzo-maror sandwich is still eaten as part of the Passover meal, though today it is meatless (since no animal

The 'Hillel Sandwich' as eaten at a modern American Passover meal: the oldest sandwich on record?

sacrifices could happen after the destruction of the Temple). The matzo is stuck together with sweet *haroset* – a nutty paste with many variants[17] – plus a dollop of horseradish standing in for the bitter herbs, again to symbolize the bitterness of slavery. The *haroset* symbolizes the mortar used by the Israelite slaves as they laboured for the Egyptians – the matzo is the bricks. But *haroset* can also stand for the sweetness of freedom (in the past it sometimes meant blood). It was Hillel's idea that Jews should taste the two flavours together, the bitter and the sweet, and the sandwich structure is the perfect vehicle for dissonant flavour combinations. In the modern version of the *Korech*, the horseradish and the *haroset* are sandwiched between two crisp slices of matzo cracker.

Hillel's original sandwich would have been different. The first matzo was essentially just a soft flatbread, like chapatti or *lavash*. The original Passover sandwich was a kind of roast lamb and herb wrap, similar to a kebab, and probably very delicious. The fact that Hillel recommended eating the meat, herbs and bread together in this way suggests that 'sandwiches' of this kind had been eaten in the Middle East for a very long time. The 'wrap', which has become so popular in the past ten years in Britain, the US and elsewhere, is sometimes viewed as a Johnny-come-lately of sandwiches. The opposite, in fact, is true. The existence of *Korech* shows that meat and vegetables encased in flatbread is of antique origin.

The Passover sandwich of the first century BC summons up an entire family of stuffed flatbreads, stretching forwards to the houmous and falafel in pitta bread eaten today throughout the Middle East, the sesame flatbreads filled with *k'nafeh* of Lebanon, the Armenian *lavash* filled with cream cheese, mint and cucumber and many more. What makes Hillel's sandwich so useful and striking for our purposes is that

A modern chicken wrap: dull descendent of a whole family of Middle Eastern flatbread sandwiches.

A sign advertising some different flavours of wrap, photographed in London's Borough Market, 2009.

WRAPS

The Greek (Giros)
Roast Pork, Tomato, Onions & Tzatziki

The Mexican
Roast Pork, Tomato, Onions & Lettuce with Salsa & Yogurt Dressing

The Turkish
Roast Pork, Tomato, Onion & Lettuce with Chili Sauce
Hot, Hot, Hot

All At £4

Hillel quite consciously and clearly introduced the notion of filling being *wrapped* or *enclosed* in bread. The word *Korech* derives from *karach*, meaning to encircle, embrace or surround. It is the same word used to denote the structure of bookbinding; as well as the enveloping of a shroud. This seems apposite. Bread in a sandwich can take on the role of a book's cover (with the filling playing the role of the leaves) or it can be a shroud which protects and covers a body of filling within.

Structurally, Hillel's sandwich is a true sandwich, the first on record. Culturally, however, it has no connection with the thing we call a 'sandwich'. This family of Middle Eastern wraps have a lineage which is entirely separate from the European sandwich; and they lack a single name to unify them.

Returning to western Europe in the centuries before the fourth Earl of Sandwich, it is very hard to find any concrete reference to ingredients being placed within bread, as opposed to being eaten alongside, or on top of it. One possible pre-sandwich is the family of spread toasts of early modern Britain, which included such toppings as veal kidney mixed with egg yolks, scrambled eggs, melted cheese and anchovies.[18] There is a reference supporting the notion of 'toasts' as precursor to the sandwich in *The European Magazine* of 1801. In a memoir of the actor Thomas Walker (1698–1744), a notorious drunk, we are told that he frequently had to eat snacks behind the scenes 'to alleviate the fumes of the liquor': these were 'Sandwiches (or, as they were then called, anchovy toasts)'. But I cannot find any reference to anchovy toasts before 1762 having a top layer of bread (though an American recipe for 'anchovy toasts' from 1847 does speak of placing the anchovies 'between the slices of toast').[19]

More broadly, there is the whole category of 'bread and something'. In an article in *Gastronomica* in 2004, Mark Morton argued that 'The sandwich appears to have been simply known as "bread and meat" or "bread and cheese".'[20] Morton rightly notes that these two phrases are found throughout English drama of the sixteenth and seventeenth centuries. In Shakespeare's *The Merry Wives of Windsor*, the character of Nim announces, 'I love not the humour of bread and cheese.' Morton notes that 'significantly' the sequence of the phrase was always 'bread and cheese' not 'cheese and bread', which could be read to suggest that the bread was being used as the foundation for the cheese, as in a sandwich.

It is hard to argue with Morton's case that 'bread and cheese' and 'bread and meat' were sometimes equivalent to the sandwich. But it is going too far to argue that 'bread and cheese' *always* meant a sandwich. Rather, then as now, 'bread and cheese' most likely meant just that – a hunk or roll of bread and a piece of cheese on a plate, which the eater could combine and eat as they saw fit. Many people must have combined cheese and bread into a 'sandwich'. Others, however, may have chosen to spear their cheese on their knife and eat it that way, or placed the cheese on a single piece of bread without adding a top layer, or munched on alternate chunks of bread and cheese.

We still lack a concrete reference to cheese or anything else being sandwiched within slices of bread in western Europe before 1762. In an anti-papal tract of 1571, *Spiritus est vicarious Christi in terra* by John Northbrooke (*fl.* 1568–1579), I have found a fleeting allusion to bread and cheese which suggests an idea of containment. Northbrooke hysterically accuses Catholics of being 'like to the Rat catchers, for they will take good bread, cheese and butter, and *within* wil put arsnecke & poison: the good bread & butter is nothing else but to allure than to eate the secrete & hidden poison, to their destruction' (my italics).[21] The insistence that the poison is 'secrete and hidden' and the idea of hiding poison *within* the bread, cheese and butter could be read to suggest a sandwich, which would be an excellent hiding place for poison. But this is no more than conjecture. It is equally possible that Northbrook is saying that the poison is secreted within the individual ingredients. Another contender is the portable 'loaves' mentioned in a cookbook of 1730 by Charles Carter (*The Complete Practical Cook*), but there are whole French loaves elaborately hollowed out and filled with meat (such as chicken or mutton) for travelling, rather than a basic sandwich in the earl's sense.

So where is the sandwich *avant la lettre*? The historian Simon Schama has suggested that the Dutch *belegde broodje* predates the sandwich, and numerous histories of the sandwich have followed him on this point. The source is a travel book of 1673 by John Ray, *Observations topographical, moral and physiological made in a journey through part of the low-countries*. Among his observations on Dutch food – Ray is fascinated by a 'green cheese, said to be coloured with the juice of sheep's dung' – Ray notes that, 'You shall seldom fail of hung Beef in any Inn you come into, which they will cut into thin slices and eat with Bread and Butter, laying the slices upon the Butter.'[22] This, argues Schama, shows that *belegde broodje* is of 'greater antiquity than the sandwich'.[23] Well, yes, except that what is being described is not a sandwich proper but an open sandwich. Ray does not say that the Dutch innkeepers added a second slice of bread of top of the meat.

As in Britain, this lack of evidence is not evidence that sandwiches were not eaten. You have only to look at the Dutch

A Dutch still life showing ham and crusty bread by Pieter Claesz. (1597–1660): an invitation to sandwich making?

still-life paintings of the sixteenth and seventeenth centuries, about which Schama writes so brilliantly, to feel sure that cheese, meat or fish stuffed into crusty bread was a basic Dutch meal. Schama writes of the ingredients of the classic still-life meal: '(not necessarily breakfast): a wedge of cheese, a loaf of bread, a herring, the ubiquitous lemon, a scattering of nuts and fruit, a roemer of Rhenish or a tankard of ale'. When you look at such paintings, the herring is begging to be crammed into the bread with a sharp squeeze of lemon. Or consider *Still Life with Roemer, Shrimp and Roll* from 1646 by Pieter Claesz. (*c.* 1597–*circa* 1661), another invitation to sandwich-making. We see a glowing glass of white wine, a crusty roll and a dish of little pink prawns. How would you eat these prawns if not in the bread? Or *Still Life with Ham* by Gerret Willemz. Heda (*c.* 1620–1702): a pink and white cooked ham on a white tablecloth with a crusty roll and some mustard. With such ingredients to hand, it would be perverse not to smear the mustard inside the roll with a slice of ham.[24]

Nevertheless, we are forced to acknowledge that before 1762, sandwiches in Europe elude the historical record, which sends us back to the conundrum of what exactly was so distinctive about the fourth earl's behaviour that he should have given his name to this basic method of eating? The answer, I would propose, is that what was new about John Montagu's sandwich – and we cannot entirely discount Grosley's reference to it as a 'new dish' in 1765/1770 – was not the fact that he ate it but the fact that he called for it ready-made. Countless anonymous others must have constructed their own sandwiches from a plate of bread and meat over the thousands of years that bread and meat were eaten. But only aristocratic Montagu – too busy to leave his desk – asked for the bread and meat to be assembled in

A construction worker pausing for a sandwich lunch on a skyscraper in New York City.

advance on his behalf, so that he would not have to stop work for even a moment. It was not the eating that was novel but the ordering. This would explain, too, how it took on his name. At venues such as the Cocoa-Tree, word would have spread fast that Montagu was ordering his cold meat ready-to-eat between two slices of bread. In this sense, he was an innovator after all, who transformed the sandwich from a humble snack into a luxury convenience food.

In *The Old Curiosity Shop*, Charles Dickens gives a little glimpse of how cumbersome sandwich-eating could have been before 1762 (and indeed continued to be in many working-class inns). The character of Kit, starving hungry, carries 'a large slice of bread and a mug of beer into a corner' and proceeds to make himself a sandwich. But in 'despatching his bread and meat', Kit manages to 'swallow two-thirds of his knife at every mouthful'. Finally, he 'incapacitated himself for further conversation by taking a most prodigious sand-wich at one bite'.[25] Dickens summons up how messy and laborious it could be turning 'bread and meat' into a sand-wich if you had to do it yourself.

By contrast, Sandwich's pre-fab sandwich was a neat thing, an architectural wonder, a meal that needed no cutlery, and yet left busy fingers free of grease. It is indeed a great invention.

2

Constructing the Sandwich

> He cut a slice of beef from the joint upon the sideboard,
> sandwiched it between two rounds of bread, and thrusting this
> rude meal into his pocket he started off upon his expedition.
>
> Arthur Conan Doyle, *The Adventures of Sherlock Holmes* (1892)

Some sandwiches are hurled together in a great hurry; others
are built with intelligent care, whether the standard two-slice
'sand-wedge', the triple-decker club, the multi-layer Scooby
Doo sandwich, the crustless triangles of hotel afternoon tea
or the asparagus pinwheel of 1970s suburbia. In any case, the
sandwich is not just food; it is a piece of engineering. The
sandwich has given its name and form to many other things,
ranging from the simple airy layers of a sandwich sponge to
the complex panelling of a 'sandwich structured composite'
used in aircraft design. But there is a certain architectural
quality in even the most elementary ham sandwich. Sand-
wich-makers – whether they are manufacturers churning out
thousands of industrial sandwiches a day or just busy mothers
assembling last-minute packed lunches – need to solve a
number of design problems, chiefly: choice of bread; how to
glue the filling to the bread without making it either soggy or
dry; whether to cut the sandwich lengthwise or diagonally;

how to get the ratio of filling to bread just right; how to transport the sandwich; and the vital question of whether to leave crusts on or off.

The earliest British sandwiches on record post-1762 emphasize thin bread and slices of cold meat. One early 'sandwich' recipe reads:

> Put some very thin slices of beef between thin slices of bread and butter; cut the ends off neatly, lay them in a dish. Veal and ham cut thin may be served in the same manner.[1]

In 1793 *Pearson's Political Dictionary* defined 'SANDWICHES' as 'Two small slices of bread and butter, almost transparent, with a thin piece of stale ham, or beef, between them'.[2]

Other early English sandwich fillings were preserved or potted fish and seafood, chiefly anchovies and potted shrimps. From the 1780s onwards, a grocer named J. Burgess

A sandwich sponge cake: one of the many foods to borrow its form from the sandwich.

based at 107 Strand, London, placed frequent advertisements in the British press, always emphasizing the excellence of his 'finest Gorgona anchovies' which he recommended 'for bread & butter, and making sandwiches'.[3] From the 1790s, a rival grocer, Mr Mackays of Soho, advertised his 'Potted shrimp . . . suitable for sandwiches'.[4]

Over the course of the nineteenth century, published sandwich fillings proliferated to take in numerous other ingredients: cheese, watercress, poultry, oysters, potted meats, nasturtium leaves, lobster, chervil and mayonnaise, salsify, pâté de foie gras, caviar, asparagus, egg and gherkin. There were sweet sandwiches, too, such as sugar with a squeeze of lemon, or (from 1886) a sandwich of stale milk rolls, golden syrup and Devonshire cream. The truth dawned that any food imaginable could be put between two slices of bread and called a sandwich. Not that it always had to be food: in a famous anecdote of the early nineteenth century, a Mrs Sawbridge, 'to show her contempt for an elderly adorer, placed the hundred pound note which he had laid upon her dressing table between two slices of bread and butter, and ate it as a sandwich'.

Marmite sarnies: sandwich construction at its most basic.

Salads and Sandwiches: the front cover of T. Herbert's book of 1890.

Over the course of the century, aristocratic sandwich-making left behind the Earl of Sandwich's basic construction, taking on refinement and sophistication. In 1890 *Salads and Sandwiches* by T. Herbert gave precise instructions on building a good sandwich. Herbert includes a vast array of fillings (in the fish section alone there are sardines and sorrel leaf, bream, carp, crab, kipper, bloater, roach and rudd, skate, trouch, tunny – 'to be bought at French provision shops' – imitation crab and lobster – 'tinned is useful') but about the fundamental construction of a sandwich Herbert is exact:

> In cutting bread one eighth of an inch is usually considered the thickness; but the thickness of the bread and quantity of the meat must be left to the maker. Butter should be used sparingly, and cayenne, salt and pepper used with a cunning hand . . .
>
> In preparing your sandwich, remember it should be pleasing to the eye and most pleasant to the taste – as delicate in appearance as possible and not one of those things one sometimes sees, which, in place of being called sandwiches, should be named mouth-distorters.[5]

This reference to 'mouth-distorters' reflects the gulf that had already opened up in sandwich construction between those eaten by the middle and upper classes as a snack – designed to be as small and dainty as possible – and those eaten by the working classes as a main meal – designed primarily to satisfy appetite as quickly as possible and therefore to be as big and filling as the bread would allow. Each posed its own challenges.

The cover of Herbert's book depicts a neat geometrical stack of square, crustless, white ham sandwiches, stacked in a block formation on a colourful china plate. You could easily eat one in a bite or two. For Herbert, in 1890, the goal of sandwich-making is to make something which is texturally as unchallenging as possible – sausage skins are to be removed, fish is best 'worked to a paste in a basin', oysters are 'chopped fine'. Yet the flavours used are exotic and stimulating. Sliced lamb is combined with 'young leaves of mints and a squeeze of lemon'. Potted beef is enlivened with cooked mushrooms, pickles and 'eschalot'. Bone marrow is 'spread like butter' and seasoned with salt, pepper and nasturtium leaves.

In the decades preceding the Second World War, upper-class sandwich fillings in Britain became ever more varied and surprising. Sandwiches for a shooting party or picnic might be relatively plain – rare roast beef and horseradish on thin white bread wrapped in greaseproof paper. For afternoon tea, however, as Arabella Boxer writes, the sandwich fillings were 'legion and quite different in character from those of today':

> Apart from a very few, like cucumber or tomato, they were made with complex mixtures of different ingredients, all finely chopped and mixed together, similar to the sandwiches we find today in cities like Vienna and Turin. Hard-boiled eggs were never simply sliced, but chopped and mixed with mayonnaise, mango chutney, or watercress. Cream cheese was combined with chopped walnuts, dates, dried apricots or stem ginger, or with honey, or redcurrant jelly.[6]

The Gentle Art of Cookery by Mrs C. F. Leyel and Miss Olga Hartley from 1947 gives a recipe for 'rose petal sandwiches', preferably made from 'bright-pink Damask or old-fashioned roses' strewn in an overlapping layer inside two slices of white bread spread with unsalted butter. *Something*

Children's sandwiches cut into fancy shapes: the more ornate side of sandwich construction.

New in Sandwiches (1933) includes some outlandish flavours, including 'cold cooked sea-kale', sliced guava, haddock and tomato sauce, cold partridge pounded with bacon and a double-decker hot sandwich called 'High Finance' made with a layer of cooked sheep's brains and parsley followed by a layer of 'diced lean ham which has been heated in seasoned gravy'. Such concoctions reflect a frenzied fear that sandwiches might be boring. This was sandwich-making to feed a jaded appetite, rather than to satisfy hunger, and it was a demanding business serving up these little morsels.

Even a sandwich with an apparently simple upper-class filling such as cucumber – a symbol of leisure, ease and privilege – took elaborate preparation to get right. In *The Importance of Being Earnest* by Oscar Wilde, the character of Algernon expresses horror that there are no cucumber sandwiches for tea – 'I ordered them specially' – when his aunt Augusta arrives. The truth is he has already eaten them all without noticing. Lane, the butler, has to explain 'gravely' that there 'were no cucumbers in the market . . . No sir, not even for ready money'. Lane is doubly put upon, given the labour that would have been required to get the sandwiches ready for tea.

First, the bread must be chosen – fine, white and a day old or it won't cut well. Next, it must be sliced ('slim as a leaf', according to the 1986 *The London Ritz Book of Afternoon Tea*)[7] and buttered. But the danger is that the bread might become so slim that it is too fragile to butter. So the cut surface of

Cucumber sandwiches: the archetypal British refined teatime sandwich, 2010 (although the cucumber slices would not satisfy Edwardian requirements for thinness).

the loaf itself must be buttered first and then sliced, piece by piece. Finally the cucumber – peeled and cut to transparent thinness – must be added. Cucumber sweats juices, particularly when salted, which threaten to wet the bread, ruining the whole construction. There are two solutions: either the sandwich must be made mere minutes before it is eaten, or the cucumber slices must be pre-sweated in a colander with salt and a little vinegar, before being carefully dried in a tea towel and pressed in a delicate layer between the bread. Finally, the crusts are removed and the sandwiches are cut – into either four little triangles or three little rectangles per round, piled up neatly on a china plate and covered with a damp cloth until teatime.

This is a far cry from the appetite-satisfying meaty sandwiches of the masses. In 1815 *The Epicure's Almanack* described the ham sandwiches sold at Evett's Ham shop in Red Lion Passage, St Giles, where 'you may purchase any quantity of ham by the pound . . . and by way of being economical, you may, if you please, put the slices thereof between the two crusts of a quartern loaf, and carry them away cool in a couple of cabbage leaves'.[8] These were very substantial sandwiches: the quartern loaf was made from exactly 3.5 pounds (1.6 kg) of wheaten flour, with a baked weight of around 4.33 pounds (2 kg), twice the size of a large modern loaf. Note, too, that, in contrast to upper-class tea sandwiches, the crusts were used.

The hearty quartern loaf was still being used for ham sandwiches in 1851. In his *London Labour and the London Poor*, Henry Mayhew described the miserable existence of ham sandwich sellers, eking out a meagre living selling sandwiches on the street. Every year in London, 436,800 of these sandwiches were consumed. The sellers would boil ham in a 'kettle', meaning a big metal pot, slice it and sandwich it between two slices of a quartern loaf with a little mustard. It was a hard life. There was no trade in wet weather, and if the sellers could not get rid of all their stock by the end of the day, there was nothing they could do with it. 'If unsold', wrote Mayhew, 'the sandwiches spoil, for the bread gets dry, and the ham loses its fresh colour; so that those who depend upon this trade are wretchedly poor.'[9]

At this basic level, sandwich construction was a constant battle between the sellers, who wanted to put as little meat in the sandwich as they could get away with, and the buyers, who were always searching for plenty of ham, to get good value for their penny sandwich (half sandwiches sold for a halfpence). One seller told Mayhew that his customers – shopkeepers and clerks, mostly – expected 'viewy' pieces of ham: ones that looked nice. 'People often want more in my sandwiches, though I'm starving on them'.[10]

Many British working-class sandwiches had no meat at all but consisted of thick doorstops of bread sandwiched with

Sandwiches being doled out to poor children in the nineteenth century, from the Szathmary Family Culinary Collection.

a little fat (as in the Yorkshire 'mucky fat' sandwich made from meat drippings) or jam. The butty, as the name suggests, was a slice of bread and butter, comparable to the German *butterbrot*. Mrs Gaskell refers to it in *North and South* in 1855 ('I ha' no buttie to give him'). Nowadays, the butty most often spoken of is the 'chip butty', a heart surgeon's nightmare, made from chips, sliced white bread and butter and sold in the chippies of the north of England to customers too skint for a portion of fish. The original butty was probably the jam butty (or 'jam-buttie'), which has been recorded in the English language since at least 1927. In Scotland, this goes by the name of the 'jeely piece', the subject of a poem by the Glasgow poet Adam McNaughtan, in which a mother hurls a jeely piece out of a low-rise tenement to her children playing outside in the street.

The jam sandwich works well as a piece of engineering, the sticky jam easily cementing the slices of bread together. The only potential problem is when the jam seeps down into the bread, something that can be avoided by spreading a waterproofing layer of butter first. The inspired children's book *The Giant Jam Sandwich* (1972) by John Vernon Lord and Janet Burroway, tells the story of how the imaginary villagers of Itching Down construct a vast jam sandwich as a wasp trap. The book portrays the jam sandwich as a wondrous piece of human craft.

For many, conversely, it has been seen as a kind of antifood, a sign of parental and culinary neglect. The jam butty has become a byword for the potential nutritional inadequacy of the sandwich, an indicator of poverty. The jam sandwich is what you eat when you can afford nothing else (hence Marks & Spencer's headline-grabbing launch of a 75p jam sandwich in 2008 to coincide with the recession). In 1948 a letter to *The Times* pointed out that 'to save a few pence a day

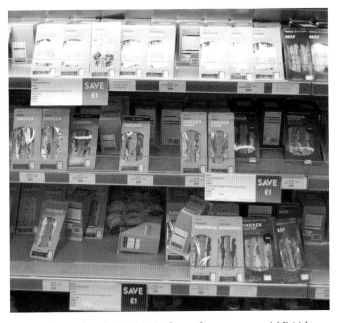

A triangular 'sand-wedge': this is the form of most commercial British sandwiches today.

some workers have adopted the practice of bringing sand-wiches, often jam sandwiches, into their works canteen'. The letter writer warned that this would result in severe 'dietetic deficiency' from a 'surfeit of carbohydrates'.[11] More recently, several schools in Britain and Australia have taken the step of banning children from bringing jam sandwiches into school for lunch.

At least the jam sandwich deceives no one, unlike many other sandwiches. With its filling hidden inside the bread, the sandwich is the perfect vehicle for fraud. Between the slices, substandard ingredients can lurk. In 2003 the Food Standards Agency in Britain announced that the practice of 'recycling' old meat in sandwiches sold at corner shops, garages and late-night stores was widespread. The swindle involved removing past-its-sell-by-date meat from sandwiches, slapping it between some fresh bread and re-labelling it with a new sell-by date. Andrew Hopkin, the chair of the task force charged with exposing the fraud, commented that 'sale or return sandwiches have become a cut-throat business and the more unscrupulous operators are resorting to extreme measures to cut costs'.[12]

In 1944 the nutritionist H. D. Renner compared the sandwich's top half to a 'coffin-lid which spells death for flavour'. He saw the sandwich as 'a poor substitute for a single slice of bread, spread with something one can both see and anticipate in advance'. The English social historian Joe Moran writes that:

> In the post-war era, the shop-bought sandwich came to stand for all that was wrong with our national cuisine and lifestyles. It was often a wretched affair of spongy, pre-sliced bread stuffed with preservatives, coated with margarine and filled with processed cheese, fish paste or luncheon meat.[13]

The badness of the post-war British sandwich became a national joke. During the years 1948–94, when the railway system was state-run, the 'British Rail sandwich' was ridiculed as all that was drab and inefficient about the country. In 2002 a thirty-year old document was dug up revealing the original British Rail catering instructions for sandwiches. It confirmed what rail travellers had always suspected: that the caterers sought to get away with the meanest portions of fillings possible. The instructions advised stacking the filling on the middle of the lower slice of bread, so that when cut in half it would seem fuller than it really was. The portion-size for a filling of luncheon meat or sardines was a negligible ⅔ ounce (20 g).[14]

At least no one died, so far as we know, from the British Rail sandwich. On an alarming number of occasions, the commercial sandwich has been implicated in food poisoning. (Marks & Spencer is said to be so careful about hygiene that sandwich workers are required to provide stool samples whenever they return from a foreign holiday, to make sure they have not picked up any nasty bugs.[15]) A research paper from 1998 published in *Epidemiology and Infection* stated that 'cold, ready-to-eat foods' – primarily the sandwich – 'are implicated most often as the source of infection in outbreaks of food borne viral gastroenteritis'.[16] Another paper from 2006 found that compared with other ready-to-eat foods, egg mayonnaise sandwiches contained 'unsatisfactory' levels of 'E.coli, S.aureus and L.monocytogenes'.[17] Even when technically clean, the sandwich has been frequently condemned on nutritional grounds. In 2008 an undercover report for Channel 4 in the UK found that some sandwiches and rolls sold by chains contained 'as much salt as 18 bags of crisps and 80 per cent more saturated fat than a Big Mac'.[18]

On the other hand, the sandwich's defenders claim that its design – which potentially combines protein, carbohydrate and vegetables in a single hand-held meal – makes it a nutritionally ideal way of eating. In 1975 the Flour Advisory Board in Britain paid for a newspaper advertisement proclaiming the dietetic virtues of the white-bread sandwich. Dr Sally Parsonage, a 'nutrition expert', was quoted as saying 'a sandwich of two slices of buttered bread, 3 oz. cheese and a sliced tomato provides as much value in protein and vitamins as a bowl of tomato soup, 3 oz. boiled gammon, gravy, peas and boiled potato'.[19] The sandwich is the foundation of one of the most famous weight-loss diets of recent years, the 'Subway diet' of Jared Fogle, who lost over 240 pounds (109 kg) on his own personal Subway diet, consisting of a 6-inch turkey sub for lunch and a foot-long veggie sub for dinner. He was subsequently employed by Subway in its ad campaigns as 'The SUBWAY® Guy'.

The fact that an entire diet could be founded on sandwiches is a sign of how entrenched the 'sandwich' has become in Western eating habits during the quarter millennium of its existence. The sandwich has given rise to numerous products specifically designed for its use. Recipes for 'sandwich spreads' date back to the nineteenth century. In 1890 the 'Household Column' in *The Manchester Times* remarked that 'tinned salmon, drained, beaten up with a fork, salt, pepper and a lump of butter mixed in with it, makes an excellent sandwich spread'.[20] In the twentieth century, sandwich spread recipes expanded to include such delicacies as mulched-up cheese, ground processed meats and flavoured cream cheese. Commercial sandwich spreads were marketed too. In 1940 Underwood Deviled Ham, an American spiced canned meat spread, marketed itself as a 'thrifty' treat for 'just-married budgets'. Even thriftier was the bottled sandwich spread – a staple food of the Depression in the 1930s – which consisted of little but vinegary mayonnaise with a few diced vegetables floating in it.

The sandwich's popularity spawned a wide range of special utensils and accessories: the silver sandwich box of the Victorians, the tin lunch pail of the pre-war American farm worker, the brown paper sandwich bag and branded lunchboxes with everything on them from Mickey Mouse to the Incredible Hulk. In 1950 lunch boxes manufactured by the Aladdin company and decorated with Hopalong Cassidy, a cowboy character, sold 600,000 in a single year. In 1953 the American Thermos Company produced a rival lunchbox

Thomas Allen, British Sandwich Maker of the Year 2009, with some of his creations.

decorated with Roy Rogers and Dale Evans, which sold 2.5 million units.[21]

Meanwhile, the rise of hot sandwiches led to a range of inventive sandwich toasters. The oldest toasted sandwich maker is probably the jaffle iron (otherwise known as pie iron or pudgy pie iron) of Australia and South Africa, a basic cast-iron clamp with a long handle which could be plunged into an outdoor camp fire or held over a gas burner. In 1974 the Australian company Breville gave the old jaffle iron a modern twist with the 'Snack 'n' Sandwich Toaster', an electric toaster with 'cut 'n' Seal mechanism' resulting in toasted sandwiches where the scorching hot fillings became effectively sealed inside. This was one of the fastest-selling small appliances in history, creating an entire school of Breville cookery. The *Breville Toasted Sandwiches Book* (1982) is a 1980s wonderland of exotica: peanut surprise, tuna treats, cheese dreams, devilled mushroom Brevilles and Alphabet Toasties, in which a can of alphabet spaghetti and a hard-boiled egg become sheathed inside the Breville's reassuring grip. More recent has been the vogue for Panini grills, which are, we are told, 'set to become the Belgian-waffle irons of the 21st century' (in other words, something we will buy like crazy for a while, only to shunt to a dusty cupboard when the craze wears off).[22]

The most important technology affected by the sandwich, however, is not a utensil, but bread itself, which has been progressively transformed to lend itself to sandwich-making, becoming softer, lighter, more geometrical and less nutritious. As early as 1851, 'sandwich loaves' were being sold. J. W. Mackie of Edinburgh advertised his 'Royal Sandwich Loaf' as enjoyed by Queen Victoria: 'Its excellence consists in being light, sweet and well-flavoured.'[23] This was followed, as Andrew F. Smith has written, by a series of revolutions in bread-making which reduced the taste and quality of bread but increased its potential for sandwich-making on a mass scale.

As Sylvester Graham (1794–1851), the evangelical temperance campaigner, complained as far back as the 1830s, the soft modern loaf was made from refined flour stripped of the brown nutritious germ. In 1892 a new bread moulding and panning machine enabled 3,600 loaves to be produced per hour. The continuous conveyor bread-baking belt (invented in 1895) allowed these loaves to be baked even faster. Then in the 1920s Gustav Papendick invented a mechanical means of slicing and wrapping bread. In Britain, in 1961, sliced bread making went over to the Chorleywood technique by which bread could be made incredibly fast – with the help of bread improvers and hardened fat. The final stage in this progressive softening of bread for sandwiches is the addition of enzymes which, thanks to a loophole in the law, do not even have to be labelled, because they are classified as a processing aid.[24] Most commercial sandwiches spend a long time in a 'cold chain'. Under normal circumstances, this would dry the bread out, but manufacturers bake the bread with added enzymes 'to help the bread and keep it springier'. The net result has been a renewed assault on the principle of crust in sandwiches, which has reached its apogee (or nadir, depending on how you look at it) in Uncrustables, a product marketed in the States by Smuckers, consisting of frozen, crustless white peanut butter and jelly sandwiches.

The archetypal soft-bread sandwich is the 'sand-wedge', pioneered in Britain by the UK department store Marks & Spencer. Sliced-bread sandwiches had been made in the home and sold in cafes, railway stations and pubs (and diners in the States) ever since the invention of sliced bread in the 1920s. But it was only in 1979 that Marks & Spencer started producing sliced-bread sandwiches, cut on the diagonal and sold from purpose-built wedge-shaped boxes. At first there were only four flavours (compared to more than seventy today). I was four in 1979, and I can still remember the deep excitement in our household when my father brought home some Marks & Spencer cream cheese and celery sandwiches to share for tea. We cut the triangles into smaller triangles and savoured every bite. The luxury! Marks & Spencer sandwiches brought the privilege of the Edwardian afternoon tea to the masses. It was like having your own butler.

The success of the Marks & Spencer sandwich was such that the luxurious connotations soon fell away. In 1991 the jeweller Gerald Ratner made a famous gaffe by joking that some of the earrings he sold were 'cheaper than an M&S prawn sandwich but probably wouldn't last as long'. The assumption was that a Marks & Spencer prawn sandwich – which the chef Simon Hopkinson has described as 'reassuringly damp', with a high volume of mayo-to-prawn – didn't cost much. By 1992 the Moorgate branch of Marks & Spencer in the City of London was selling 3 million sandwiches a year, with fillings including chicken tikka, bacon and avocado and Wensleydale and chutney. Marks & Spencer soon had rivals in the 'sand-wedge' market including Boots the chemist, which sold slimming sandwiches alongside outré flavours such as duck and orange; and Pret A Manger, which distinguished itself by making all of its sandwiches fresh in the store. Pret has played with the basic form of the sand-wedge, offering slender half sandwiches ('Slim Pret') and even, for a few years, reclassifying its salads as 'no-bread sandwiches', as if all food could be defined in relation to sandwiches. Its fillings advertise their specialness (and, by implication, that of their clientele): 'Wild Crayfish and Rocket', 'Award-winning Avocado and Herb Salad Wrap'. Bacon is 'beech-smoked'. Salmon Niçoise is 'sustainable'. (Pret are currently examining their policy on tuna – it may soon cease to be sold by them.)

Compared to the 1850s, when the sandwiches for sale on the streets of London were ham, ham or ham, the variety of affordable sandwich fillings is immense. But this illusion of choice disguises the fundamental sameness of the commercial sandwich: no matter what exotica the average sand-wedge

A solution to the problem of holding a sandwich and a drink while still leaving one hand free: the Ideal Home Exhibition, 1963.

is filled with, it will still be damp, insubstantial and a little depressing. Mayonnaise, once a sign of luxury – a recipe for lobster sandwiches from 1890 includes a whole pint of 'best Lucca olive oil' for making the mayonnaise to coat the lobster meat – has become a signal of low quality, just another way of cutting corners. The industry standard for mayo-based fillings is 50 per cent mayo to tuna or mayo to chicken, which adds yet more wetness to the already damp, spongy bread. There is now a total reversal of the nineteenth-century situation, when crust was for the masses and crustless was for the upper-crust. Now, the most expensive and desirable sandwiches are made in independent delis and cafes from crusty artisanal bread stuffed with chewy fillings such as prosciutto and wild rocket, or buffalo mozzarella and fennel salami.

The distaste for crust, moreover, has had an unfortunate side-effect in the form of colossal waste. In 1933 M. Redington White, the author of *Something New in Sandwiches*, devoted much thrifty attention to avoiding the problem of waste.

'Trim all sandwiches before filling' was the advice. 'Trimmings can then be used in other ways': in bread sauce, summer pudding or meat loaf, for example.²⁵ The trimmings from the modern sand-wedge are seldom so usefully employed. In 2009, in his book *Waste*, Tristram Stuart stated that Marks & Spencer's 'absurdly strict aesthetic requirements force one of its major sandwich suppliers to throw away four slices of bread for every loaf it uses – the crust and the first slice at either end – amounting to around 17 per cent of each loaf, or 13,000 slices from a single factory every single day'.²⁶

Sandwich construction: making porchetta sandwiches in Italy, 1957.

Crusts left over from sandwich-making.

This is before we even get to the widespread problem at sandwich shops of countless perfectly edible sandwiches being discarded at the end of each day. Waste affects all food, but particularly sandwiches because they are so perishable: a day-old sandwich is generally unsaleable. In a book aimed at trade readers, Sandwich Bar owner Stephen Miller offers some tips on how independent café owners could minimize sandwich waste: use the leftover sandwiches for children's packed lunches; invite friends round for an 'impromptu sandwich supper'; come to an arrangement with a local homeless charity and donate leftovers; or if all else fails use leftover crusts as an excuse for a walk and feed the birds: 'My favourite thing is getting the seagulls to catch rolled up bits of bread in mid air!'[27]

Waste aside, the sandwich has proved to be a remarkably versatile piece of design. It can be built up vertically, as in the American club, triple decker and Dagwood sandwiches. Or it can be expanded horizontally, as in the record-breaking sandwich made by a group of New York chefs in 1970, measuring 1,058 feet, 10 inches (322.73 metres) long, about a fifth of a mile; the filling included 80 pounds (36 kg) of liverwurst, 100 pounds (45 kg) of ham, 40 pounds (18 kg) each of salami and bologna and 5,000 slices of tomato. Conversely, the sandwich can be rendered tiny and decorative, as in the children's sandwiches cut into pretty animal shapes, popular in Japan. Square sandwiches can be piled up on a cake stand, or laid out geometrically in a 'chequerboard' effect: brown-white-brown-white. The sandwich can also become cylindrical. Rolled sandwiches (with their spin-off, the pin-wheel), in which the filling is rolled inside the bread, go back to the late nineteenth century.

Other variants of sandwich design are those in which an entire loaf is hollowed out and used as a receptacle. These include: *Pan Bagnat* from Nice (a crusty loaf filled with anchovies or tuna, tomatoes and olives), Muffaletta from New Orleans (a large Sicilian loaf filled with layers of a special olive salad

A ridiculously large sandwich, 1978.

A Muffaletta from New Orleans: one of the family of sandwiches in which an entire loaf is hollowed out and filled, in this case with cured meats and olive salad.

made with celery and cauliflower and capicola, salami, mortadella, emmentaler and provolone), the 'book-maker's sandwich' (a mammoth construction of cold steak and mustard in a Vienna loaf, eaten by the Irish at race-meetings) and the 'shooter's sandwich' (a whole fillet steak, mushrooms, salt and pepper inside a hollow long loaf, weighted down overnight between two chopping boards so that the meat juices seep into the bread). Food writer Tim Hayward, who likes to add caramelized shallots, 'a shot of brandy and a splash of Worcestershire sauce' to the steak, deems the shooter's sandwich 'a triumph of Edwardian cuisine'.[28] Most bizarre are the 'sandwich loaves' of mid-twentieth century America, where a whole loaf is sliced in many horizontal layers, before being filled (with tuna mayo, perhaps, or Cheez Whiz, a processed cheese spread) and frosted with cream cheese, like a cake. It is then sliced and eaten, in suburbia, with a fork.

These gargantuan creations show how the sandwich has gone far beyond the earl's original requirement of a simple hand-held meal. Many sandwiches now are too vast either for hand or mouth to contain. The eater is forced to deconstruct the sandwich into its constituent parts before it can be eaten, which, as the food writer Alan Davidson once remarked, rather defeats the purpose.

3
Who Eats Sandwiches?

'What are them clerks eating Sandvidges for?' asked Mr Weller,
senior, of his son, Sam, when they went together to the
Will Office, at the Bank of England. 'Cos it's their dooty,
I suppose,' replied Sam, 'it's a part of the system: they're
allvays a-doin' it here, all day long.'
Charles Dickens, *The Pickwick Papers* (1836–7)

The sandwich is unusual in that it has always been both poor
food and rich food – and middling food to boot. Unlike pizza,
which was once peasant food but became gentrified, or roast
chicken, a mass-market food that used to be elite, the sandwich
has always belonged to all classes and ages of society. Right
from the earliest years after the word entered the language in
Britain, the 'sandwich' was eaten by people of every profession – or no profession – in numerous settings where a formal
meal with a knife and fork wouldn't fit the bill. An observer
of the household of King George III noted in 1789 that the
royal family 'never fail to carry' sandwiches with them, going
on to describe the King and Queen having sandwiches on board
a boat.[1] In 1813 *The European Magazine* referred to the Princess
of Wales ordering some sandwiches.[2] Yet sandwiches were also
hearty tavern food, eaten by the humblest citizens of the land.

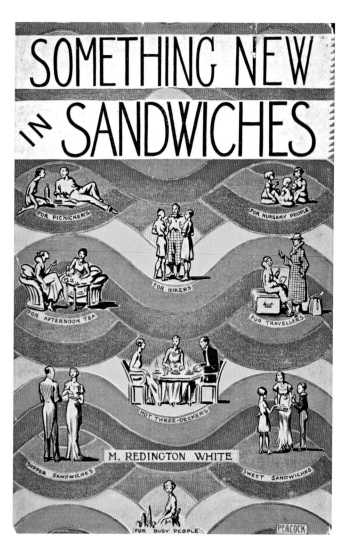

Front cover of *Something New in Sandwiches*, 1933, by M. Redington White, showing the range of different people who ate sandwiches.

Afternoon tea at the Lanesborough Hotel, London, continuing the grand tradition of finger sandwiches.

The nature of the sandwiches varied drastically according to who was eating them, and when. Among the upper classes, as Gibbon's diary entry from 1762 suggests, sandwiches were dainty supper food, whether alone or eaten in combination with other titbits. In 1773, in a book of 'Bill of Fares', Charlotte Mason includes sandwiches as part of an elaborate-sounding supper comprising two small chickens, fricasséed, crab, sweetmeats, cheesecakes, snipes, floating islands of chocolate, house lamb's fry, tartlets, sweetmeats, small hare and finally sandwiches.[3] In such a genteel setting, sandwiches can have been little more than a slight supper-time snack, a little treat before bedtime. In 1797 Henry James Pye writes of 'that unsocial substitute for supper, sandwiches and wine brought round in a salver'.[4] Similarly, a novel from 1793, *Louisa Matthews*, refers to ladies eating 'a very slight repast of salad and sandwiches' at 'supper-time'.[5]

As well as being served at supper time, they were also provided as a kind of elevenses in the morning, between breakfast and lunch. In 1802 *The Times* told an anecdote about a farmer's daughter going to visit 'a family of some fashion in Essex', noting that 'as her visit was a morning one, sandwiches were introduced'.[6] For such fashionable families, sandwiches were a superfluous little nicety, a supplement to other meals.

By contrast, for the working classes, the sandwich – hunks of bread and meat or cheese – was the meal itself, and you were lucky to get it. Dickens's *Little Dorrit* (1857) speaks of 'midday when a glass of sherry and a humble sandwich of whatever cold meat in the larder might not come amiss'.[7] Dickens also gives a fantastical account of a sandwich being eaten by a tall lady, as told by one of the characters in *The Pickwick Papers* (1836–7), who lamented the low archway at a coach yard:

> Terrible place – dangerous work – other day – five children – mother – tall lady, eating sandwiches – forgot the arch – crash – knock – children look round – mother's head off – sandwich in her hand – no mouth to put it in – head of a family off – shocking, shocking.

Although this is a comedy, it gives an all-too-vivid sense of sandwiches as the food of people on the move, street food, something to munch while strolling along daydreaming or to snatch whenever time allowed.

Sandwiches were the food of travel, too. In 1789 the grocer John Burgess advised buying his finest 'Gorgona anchovies . . . for making sandwiches' for 'families going into the country'. Sandwiches were what travellers ate, either on their journey or when they arrived at their destination, too

Sandwiches as the food of poverty: 'The Big Hand-out Hobo Convention',
Cincinnati, some time between 1910 and 1915.

late for dinner. In *Jane Eyre*, when our heroine first arrives at
Thornfield (home of Mr Rochester) after a long journey,
Mrs Fairfax asks Leah to 'make a little hot negus and cut a
sandwich or two'. In both Britain and the United States, sandwiches were intimately associated with the new railways.
'During the early years of the railroad,' says the *Encyclopedia
of Food and Culture* (2003), 'sandwiches proved an ideal form
of fast food, especially since it could be sold at train stations
when everyone got off to buy snacks.' With a captive market,
station sandwiches were not always the most delicious. A letter
to *The Times* in 1883 complained about the new refreshment
rooms at Swindon serving 'stale sandwiches and Banbury
cakes at 6d each'.[8] During the First World War, there was a
convention for serving free sandwiches at railway stations
to soldiers travelling on duty. In these desperately hungry
times, the doling out of free food had evidently caused

Sandwiches as the food of travel: a Canadian air stewardess offers an appealing tray of 'cocktail sandwiches'.

some complaint, for on 5 February 1918 a May Limberick felt the need to write to *The Times* defending the practice:

> Each man served is a bona-fide traveller, and must show his pass or ticket before being served. The [sandwiches] contain ¼ oz of bread, thinly spread with tinned meat,

which is minced and mixed with potatoes. These meat sandwiches are only given between the hours of 12 noon and 2pm, and again after 6pm. Each man is allowed one sandwich, but men leaving for overseas . . . are allowed an extra sandwich when asked for.[9]

The last detail is particularly heart-rending. Limberick concludes that many of these soldiers were 'wounded and stretcher cases' who were 'greatly cheered by the hospitality'.

Whether in times of war or peace, sandwiches were the ideal food to plug the gap between official meal times. They have a long connection with the theatre, providing a solution to the problem of how to fit in an evening meal around a theatrical performance, both for performers and audience. On 15 May 1788 a thespian group including the playwright Richard Sheridan, Mrs Sheridan and the Duchess of Devonshire had

A wounded soldier being handed a reviving sandwich during the First World War.

a little supper following some theatricals consisting of 'Beef, sandwiches, Porter etc.'[10] That same year, an audience at the Wargrave Theatre London was served with 'cakes, sandwiches, wines etc. etc.' in the interval between a play and a farce.[11]

The ham-sandwich sellers interviewed by Henry Mayhew in 1851 got much of their business from theatres, touting their wares 'at Ashley's, the Surrey and the Vic' as well as the ''lympic' and the 'Delphi' (the Olympic and the Adelphi):

> The ham-sandwich seller carries his sandwiches on a tray or flat basket, covered with a clean white cloth; he also wears a white apron, and white sleeves. His usual trade is at the doors of the theatres.[12]

One of the sandwich sellers told Mayhew he was out until four in the morning, catering for people pouring out of the theatres and the 'night-houses'. His customers were often drunk and rude. 'Six times I've been upset by drunken fellows, on purpose, I've no doubt, and lost all my stock.'

From the customer's perspective, however, the easy availability of the sandwich was a great boon, a way of getting through an evening of entertainment without ever getting hungry. Here is Dickens again, in *The Uncommercial Traveller*, showing how sandwiches could feature at every stage of an evening at the theatre, before, during and after the play:

> Between the pieces . . . crowds of us had sandwiches and ginger-beer at the refreshment-bars established for us in the Theatre. The sandwich – as substantial as was consistent with portability, and as cheap as possible – we hailed as one of our greatest institutions. It forced its way among us at all stages of the entertainment, and we were always delighted to see it; its adaptability to the varying moods of

our nature was surprising; we could never weep so comfortably as when our tears fell on our sandwich; we could never laugh so heartily as when we choked with sandwich; Virtue never looked so beautiful or Vice so deformed as when we paused, sandwich in hand, to consider what would come of that resolution of Wickedness in boots, to sever Innocence in flowered chintz from Honest Industry in striped stockings. When the curtain fell for the night, we still fell back upon sandwich, to help us through the rain and mire, and home to bed.

The theatre was just one of many leisure activities which came to depend on the sandwich for smooth running. Sandwiches were brought to sporting events, as food for athletes and as food for spectators. In 1804 a crew of six London watermen rowed against six Gravesend watermen. The men of each boat, reported *The Times*, were 'provided with sandwiches of cold fowl, and brandy & water, in bottles'.[13] Sandwiches were gambling food too, in keeping with the myth of their origin. Gaming houses tended to supply sandwiches free of charge, as a way of encouraging gamblers to stay for longer and lose more money.[14]

More wholesomely, sandwiches were – and are – the food par excellence of picnics. They could be wrapped in a damp cloth or, later, waxed or greaseproof paper, and put in a hamper, box or basket ready for an outdoors jaunt. By the 1880s the terms 'sandwich case' and 'picnic case' were being used interchangeably.[15] Sandwiches were enjoyed on every kind of picnic, from the grand country house picnics on the river (at which sandwiches accompanied salads, cold hams and cakes) to the simple impromptu meals of day trippers. In 1882 one day tripper observed that 'the people have brought their sandwiches with them' when visiting the Crystal Palace

Some happy picnickers enjoying sandwiches.

in London 'for some 28 years' (protesting at a new notice forbidding visitors to bring any provisions to the palace).[16] In the 1920s sandwiches became associated with the rising vogue for hiking. In 1929 Florence A. Cowles recommended bacon sandwiches as 'particularly good on hikes or picnics'.

Sandwiches and picnics are synonymous. In *Good Sandwiches and Picnic Dishes* (1948), Ambrose Heath wrote that 'when we think of a picnic, it is the sandwich that first generally springs to mind'. Heath praises the 'delectably gritty sandwiches' of a beach picnic, where sand has got into the picnic basket. From the same era, Enid Blyton's *Famous Five* novels for children are full of the joys of outdoor sandwiches: 'Pass the sandwiches, Anne, the tomato ones, golly!' The eponymous 'five' eat 'Egg and sardine sandwiches, tomato and lettuce, ham – there seemed no end of them!' In one story, *Five on a Secret Trail*, their aunt 'cuts' them 'dozens and dozens of sandwiches' to take on an adventure. 'She said if we kept them in this tin they wouldn't go stale', remarks Anne, the most domestic of the five. 'They sat out in the sun, munching ham sandwiches. Anne had brought tomatoes too, and they took a bite at a sandwich and then a bite at a tomato.' Bliss.

As Enid Blyton knew, sandwiches have a particular association with children. Those who take a packed lunch to school every day can easily eat in the region of two hundred sandwiches a year, more if they occasionally have them for supper too. Andrew F. Smith remarks that the invention of sliced bread in the 1920s cemented the relationship between children and sandwiches, because now they could make a sandwich for themselves without any worries about sharp knives. This is doubtless true; but sandwiches were considered children's food long before the invention of the slicing machine. 'Does your little one go to school and take a lunch?' asked the *New York American* on 6 April 1898. 'If so, prepare a club sandwich for the luncheon basket'.[17]

A toddler's bento box lunch.

In 1880 the 'Household Column' of the *Manchester Times* recommended sandwiches for 'children's supper parties': 'Nice sandwiches can be made of finely chopped tongue or watercress minced.' Similarly, in 1903 a column called 'The World of Women' in *The Penny Illustrated Newspaper* advised that for a children's party you should 'have sandwiches, no cucumber or cress – little children do not like them'. This opinion, which is quite untrue in my experience (or at least no more true of children than it is of adults), prevails to this day. In 2009 the sandwich chain Pret a Manger launched a range of 'kids' sandwiches', which were like the grown-up versions but without any greenery: 'Kids Free Range Egg & Mayo' (without any cress); 'Kids Pole & Line Caught Tuna' (without any cucumber). Certain fillings have a particular affinity with children: peanut butter and jelly in America, for example, or the sandwiches of sugar or hundreds and thousands (sprinkles) sometimes made in British homes as a great

American women eating sandwiches on a bench, Manhattan.

and furtive treat. (In Australia, this is known as fairy bread, but is served open, not sandwiched.)

At the opposite end of the spectrum, sandwiches can be a very grown-up and rather pleasureless affair: an on-duty rather than off-duty food. No dish has a stronger association with the world of work, from the fourth earl hard at work at his desk at the Admiralty onwards. Sandwiches have fuelled the entire British parliamentary system. In 1793 Joseph Pearson, the great observer of the political scene of Whitehall, claimed that in the House of Commons, sandwiches were used to

> keep the people in the gallery from famishing, from Eleven o' clock, till six the next morning. – n.b. Bellamy charges a shilling for them, and they don't stand him in above twopence. I once had one from him, and his wife made me pay for it.[18]

Sandwiches were eaten by MPs too, who gobbled them down in odd moments between sessions. In 1852 *The Times* lamented the problem of MPs dining. On the one hand, it was undesirable that they should linger over dinner with friends or at clubs, where they were liable to stay too long and miss important votes. On the other, 'they should dine and dine well' and not be forced to bring into the chamber 'in their pockets a German sausage or a case of ham sandwiches, and devour them in their places. Even patriotism has its limits.'[19]

Sandwiches were important in the law courts too. In the London court reporting of the nineteenth century, there are several cases of jurors becoming tired, hungry or sick over the course of a long deliberation and being revived with sandwiches and wine or sherry.[20] Sandwiches also fuel modern lawsuits and lawyers. From the long hours of law school to the even longer hours of legal practice, sandwiches enable the lawyer's obsession with work to continue uninterrupted. There's a joke, origin unknown, about the need of lawyers to carry sandwiches with them at all times. Two lawyers walk into a bar and order drinks. Then they open their briefcases and produce sandwiches. The bartender angrily objects: 'You can't eat your own sandwiches in here!' The two lawyers shrug and exchange sandwiches with each other.

It's a reminder of how essential sandwiches are to the working day. The sandwiches of leisure have a rather feminine overtone: afternoon tea is a ladylike institution. By contrast, the early sandwich bars could be masculine, serving men and their work. In Glasgow in the 1880s, according to Perilla Kinchin (in a book on Mackintosh, the Art Nouveau architect), these bars developed 'to meet the needs of men'. At Lang's in Glasgow, which opened in the mid-nineteenth century to meet the need for food in a man's lengthening working day,

> customers, male only, helped themselves to milk, ales, whisky, and a staggering variety of sandwiches, pies and pastries, for which they paid on an honour system that worked perfectly until the Second World War. They always stood and kept their hats on, as if to demonstrate that they were not really stopping for lunch.[21]

The workplace has changed dramatically – hats, men-only offices and whisky in the middle of the day are all out of fashion – but we are still not really stopping for lunch. According to the social historian Joe Moran, seven out of ten workers in Britain now practise 'desk-dining, the average time taken to eat their lunch in front of the computer being 3.5 minutes'. What this means, in practice, is that most people are gobbling down a sandwich as fast as they can. Even the most basic of salads takes longer than 3.5 minutes to eat: you might have to put down your fork from time to time or actually pause to cut an unwieldy lettuce leaf. But a sandwich can be applied to face and devoured in a trice.

4
The American Sandwich

The sandwiches are elaborate affairs
Toast, bacon, toast, chicken, toast
Charles Reznikoff, *Rhythms II* (1919)

America took sandwiches and made them something else – 'elaborate affairs' indeed, in the words of the objectivist poet Charles Reznikoff. Like skyscrapers, their construction was ambitiously and generously vertical: 'toast, bacon, toast, chicken, toast'. As Florence Cowles wrote in *Seven Hundred Sandwiches* (1929), the challenge was to stack up the layers without making them 'topply'. In Britain, as we have seen, the most elaborate pre-war upper-class sandwiches were very tiny, designed to be swallowed in a single bite. By contrast, from the 1890s onwards, American elaboration made the sandwich a much larger and more enthusiastic construction than the fourth earl's original beef sandwich. Sandwiches, even when consumed as part of a working day, were no longer an austere means to an end – eating as fast as possible – but a glorious and greedy end in themselves. Two slices of bread became three slices, four slices, or more. The often dull filled rolls of Britain were transformed lengthwise into hoagies, torpedoes and subs. And American sandwiches were personified with names: Reuben, BLT, Elvis Special, Monte Cristo.

The original American sandwiches of the early to mid-nineteenth century were probably fairly similar to what was being eaten across the Atlantic. Sandwich recipes were first mentioned in American cookbooks as early as 1816. In 1840 Eliza Leslie gave a recipe for a ham sandwich which would not have looked out of place in London society:

> Cut some thin slices of bread very neatly, having slightly buttered them; and, if you choose, spread on a very little mustard. Have ready some very thin slices of cold boiled ham, and lay one between two slices of bread. You may either roll them up, or lay them flat on the plates. They are used at supper, or at luncheon.[1]

Similarly, in 1866 Mrs Crowen writes of plain 'bread and butter sandwiches' made of 'cold meat sliced thin' and in

A multi-layer sandwich as eaten in the Hanna-Barbera cartoon *Scooby-Doo*.

Club sandwiches by Wayne Thiebaud.

1869 Mrs Putnam suggests ham or tongue cut 'very thin' laid 'smoothly' on thin bread buttered 'with nice butter'.[2] She advises trimming 'off the edges, that the sandwiches may be all one size'. These dry, plain, small sandwiches are entirely in keeping with British sandwiches of the same period.

By the turn of the century, however, American fancy sandwiches were diverging from those of Britain. Fillings were gussied up with mayonnaise. And sandwiches were no longer named solely according to their component parts: ham sandwich, cheese sandwich and so on. Possibly starting with the 'club sandwich', American sandwiches were dignified with proper names.

The exact origins of the club sandwich are unknown. Some say it was first made in 1894 in the kitchens of the Saratoga Club, a casino in New York. Others suggest it may have originated in 1895 on the club-cars of the us railroad. Another explanation is that it originated at home. In 1916, when the club sandwich was still just about a novelty, Marion H. Neil told the legend of it being created when a man returned home from his club one night 'after the family and servants had retired' and ransacked the pantry for something to eat. He found butter, mayonnaise, a tomato, some cold chicken and cold cooked bacon, oddments which he layered between two slices of toast.[3] In other words, in this account, the club sandwich was an early example of what Jane and Michael Stern have called 'the ever-popular what's-in-the-refrigerator?-on-white'.[4]

Whether Neil's story is true or false, what's striking about the club sandwich described is that it has only two layers of bread – or rather, toast – and not three. The earliest 'club sandwiches' on record, from the 1890s, were composed of white meat from a roast chicken, bacon, crisp lettuce and/or tomato all sandwiched between two slices of toasted buttered white bread. What was new about it was not the number of slices of bread but the particular combination of ingredients and the fact that it was both hot (toast, bacon) and cold (lettuce/tomato, mayonnaise, chicken). In 1900 *The Boston Globe* still found the addition of cold mayonnaise to hot bacon 'rather startling'.[5]

On the other hand, there was something called a 'club house' sandwich and this did indeed have three – or more – layers of bread. The first published recipe for it is in Sarah Tyler Rorer's *Sandwiches* in 1894. In 1914 'The Neighbourhood Cook Book' by the Council of Jewish Women in Portland, Oregon gave a recipe for 'Club House sandwiches' involving no fewer than four slices:

Toast thin slices of white bread, butter them lightly and place on them thin slices of crisp fried bacon. Lay on another slice of buttered toast, then slices of chicken well seasoned, another slice of toast and then cucumbers, pickles sliced crosswise and another slice of toast.[6]

Over time, the club house sandwich and the club sandwich became one and the same. By 1928 Florence A. Cowles, who gave no fewer than seventeen different versions of the club sandwich, stated that 'The club sandwich may consist of anywhere from one to five stories. The foundation is always toast, but the superstructure depends on the maker's fancy – and the materials at hand.'[7] She even gives a recipe for a Russian club sandwich (see Recipes) in which an entire five-course meal is constructed between six slices of bread.

The club sandwich, like all the great American sandwiches, has inspired fierce passions. In 1930 the US Congress debated in the most heated terms the size, quality and price of the club sandwich served in the cafeteria of the House of Representatives. The pretext was a recent bill asking for $30,000 to subsidize the House restaurant. Mr Murphy of Ohio stood up to protest this bill, angrily waving two club sandwiches, 'red-faced and shaking'. Murphy argued that it was an outrage that the restaurant should be asking for a subsidy when it charged the exorbitant sum of 70 cents for a club sandwich, a price not exceeded by the swankiest Washington hotel. He extracted the piece of chicken from the House club sandwich and held it up to show that it was not worth the price. Many murmured assent with Murphy. But the representative for Alabama chipped in, 'I have heard a lot about club sandwiches, but what about those of us who can't afford club sandwiches and don't eat them? What about ham sandwiches?'[8]

In Depression-era America, sandwiches were a basic working-class food, bought from luncheonettes, five-and-dimes and grocery stores as well as being quickly assembled at home from newfangled sliced white bread. Sandwiches were a key menu item at the 'diners' which started in Providence, Rhode Island, in 1872. Every item cost a nickel. Diner historian Richard Gutman writes of the '"chewed" sandwich served at the very first diner (which was nothing more than a horse-drawn wagon, selling boiled eggs, pies, sandwiches and coffee), consisting of scraps left over on the cutting board, chopped still finer, and spread with butter and mustard between two slices of bread'.[9] As lunch wagons moved off the streets and became fixed places, the sandwich menu expanded. In diner jargon, you could order a sandwich 'all the way' (with lettuce, mayonnaise, onion and butter) or 'high and dry' (with no butter, mayonnaise or lettuce).[10] Particular diners developed house specialities, such as the Trilby sandwich served at the White House Café in Waterbury, Connecticut (minced ham

Cheap food: American children in 1939 enjoying a thrifty snack of margarine on sliced bread, in an advertisement for Nucoa margarine.

Al's Sandwich Shop, Miami Beach, Florida.

and a slice of Bermuda onion).[11] Above all, the diner sandwich was cheap. In 1932, at the Worcester Lunch Car in Newburyport, Massachusetts, 10 cents would buy you any of the following sandwiches: cream cheese and olive, cream cheese and jelly, cold sliced ham, cold minced ham, grilled hamburg (in other words a hamburger), or American cheese. If you wanted the bread toasted, that was 5 cents extra.[12]

The story of Bonnie Parker (1910–1934) and Clyde Barrow (1909–1934) – otherwise known as Bonnie and Clyde – gives a little snapshot of what a poor life sustained on sandwiches might look like. Jeff Guinn, biographer of Bonnie and Clyde, writes that their 'entire menu' while on the run often comprised 'bologna-and-cheese sandwiches', sometimes supplemented with a glass of buttermilk.[13] Bologna, also known as baloney – pale pink luncheon meat – was often pretty unwholesome stuff. American meatpackers used 'bologna' as shorthand for meat that was so substandard it was only fit for sausages. Still, it was filling, and remarkably economical. Bonnie and Clyde bought sandwiches for breakfast on the very morning that they were finally apprehended and shot by the police. Opinion differs as to whether their final sandwich, bought from Ma Canfield's café in Gibsland, Louisiana, was a fried bologna or a BLT. But the remains of Bonnie's sandwich was still on her lap when she was killed, wrapped neatly in a paper napkin.[14]

It's worth noting that Bonnie and Clyde saw sandwiches as a breakfast food. In Britain the choice of breakfast sandwiches is essentially limited to the 'greasy spoon' bacon or sausage sarnie (though some cafes do now do Panini filled with an all-day British breakfast of egg and bacon). In America, however, breakfast sandwiches are plenteous and varied. The repertoire of morning sandwiches was built up first through diners and street vendors. It includes the classic bacon and egg roll; toasted sandwiches of peanut butter and bacon; soft breakfast burritos stuffed with green pepper omelette; Tex-Mex sandwiches of avocado and salsa; and the McDonald's Egg McMuffin, in which an eerily round fried egg made in a Teflon ring is stacked inside an English muffin with melted cheese and a slice of Canadian bacon (first served in California in 1972).

In their book *Roadfood Sandwiches* (2007), in which they travel the States for no other purpose than to eat the best sandwiches, Jane and Michael Stern describe the joy of a breakfast sandwich bought from a little street cart called Tony's, in New York City, which parks at Nassau and Wall Street from around 4 a.m. The eggs are cracked fresh for every order and cooked on a tiny griddle. The Sterns order Bacon and Egg on a long roll: 'a magnificent lode of buttery eggs and sizzled bacon folded inside a muscular hero roll with a silky seeded crust'. They note that, unlike bacon and egg rolls eaten elsewhere in the States, this one is served on 'a tubular

A kitsch American sandwich made from fried egg and canned asparagus on toast.

The Reuben, a classic American overstuffed sandwich.

length of bread that has real muscle – less a matter of crust than of chew'.[15]

This brings us to another crucial facet of the sandwich in America: its extreme regional variation. Popular sandwiches vary not just from state to state but from district to district – or even from diner to diner – and the construction of any given regional sandwich is guarded with patriotic jealousy.

A good example is the hoagie, an oblong Italian-American roll stuffed with multiple layers of cold meats, cheese, lettuce and condiments. Depending on where in the States you eat one, it may go under the name of blimpie, bomber, grinder, wedge, zeppelin or zep, Cuban sandwich, poor boy or po'boy, rich girl, rocket, gondola, spucket, torpedo, tunnel, rocket, sub, or simply 'Italian sandwich', and the composition will vary significantly from place to place. The 'wedge', served between two wedges of bread, is specific to Westchester County, New York. The Louisiana po'boy centres on seafood, whereas the

A hoagie (aka sub, aka zep).

grinders and zeps of the East Coast are meat-based. The New York hero – so named in the 1930s because you need a heroic appetite to finish one – usually features a single cold meat, whereas the Philadelphia hoagie will have many types (for example prosciutto, coppa and sopressata).

Fiercely competing foundation myths attach to each of the variants. Take the hoagie itself, eaten by Italian immigrants in South Philadelphia from the early twentieth century onwards: some say the name comes from Hog Island, the shipyard where the Italians mostly worked. Others suggest that the name comes from the fact that you would have to be a 'hog' to eat a whole 8-inch roll stuffed with salami and provolone. Al de Palma, who ran the sandwich shop that claimed to serve the first hoagie in 1936, called them 'hoggies'.[16] But in 1984 a Mrs Antoinette Iannelli of Maine told the *New York Times* that she and not Mr de Palma had served the first hoagie in Philadelphia. Around 1934, a police officer came to her food stand saying he had argued with his wife, and asked her to make him a sandwich:

> She cut a loaf of Italian bread in half, she said, packed it with meats, olives, onions, lettuce and tomatoes and mixed a sauce to keep it moist. 'Lo and behold,' said Mrs Iannelli, 'that was it. The next day that policeman was back saying "Antoinette, fix me one of those sandwiches for the captain."'[17]

However, the historian of Philadelphian food, William Woys Weaver, argues that the name hoagie derives from 'hokey-pokey', the name of a cheap form of ice cream sold by 'hokey-pokey men' on the streets of Philadelphia.[18] Perhaps these vendors sold hoagies on the side; or ate them.

There is no real hope of getting to the bottom of these rival stories. The fact that such arguments persist is best seen as a sign of the deep affection generated by local sandwiches. You could find similar disputes about the origin of the Philly cheesesteak (hot sliced steak and onions inside a hoagie with either Cheez Whiz or a slice of processed cheese), the Western or Denver sandwich (scrambled eggs, ham, pepper and onions in a roll), the BLT (bacon, lettuce and tomato) and the PBJ (peanut butter and jelly). The Reuben, a deli special made from corned beef, sauerkraut and cheese on rye bread, is the subject of vicious disputes between those who insist it was invented in New York by deli owner Arnold Reuben and those who claim it was first made by Reuben Kulakofsky of the Blackstone Hotel, Omaha, Nebraska.

The American sandwiches which are easiest to pin down are those connected with a specific place or person, like the 'Elvis sandwiches' of mashed bananas and peanut butter in white bread fried in butter, known to have been eaten by the singer at any time of day or night. Another sandwich with a very specific lineage is the Dagwood, also known as the Skyscraper Special, first mentioned on 16 April 1936 in the *Blondie* cartoon strip by Murat 'Chic' Young. The character of Dagwood Bumstead (Blondie's husband) goes to the fridge and builds a sandwich from anything he can find: tongue, onions, mustard, sardines, beans, horseradish. Over the years, the sandwiches fashioned by Dagwood became ever more ridiculous, a mishmash of utterly incompatible ingredients. In 1944 his sandwiches become so unwieldy, he decides to take an electric drill to them and 'dowel them together with a frankfurter'.[19]

Unfortunately, the joke was frequently lost on Dagwood's audience. The Dagwood sandwich is served and eaten in all seriousness. It has become part of a great American tradition of vertical sandwiches. On the one hand, there are such things as the Muffaletta, that delicious New Orleans speciality in which layers of piquant olive salad and cold meats are placed inside an entire hollowed-out loaf, or the oyster loaf, where cooked oysters similarly fill out a hollow roll. There is a certain integrity to these sandwiches. On the other hand, there are the Scooby-Doo-style sandwiches where any ambition to fit one inside a human mouth is futile. One variant is the Fresser, served at D. Z. Akins in San Diego, California. The name comes from the Yiddish 'fresser', meaning 'one who eats': as many as sixteen slices of deli meats (pastrami-roast turkey-corned beef-roast beef and so on) plus cheese and tomato are delicately balanced between two thin slices of rye bread and held in place with long wooden skewers.

Even Jane and Michael Stern, whose appetite for American sandwiches is almost limitless, express a little exasperation in the face of such towers of food:

A boy trying and failing to get his mouth around a mammoth skyscraper sandwich.

These creations grow so tall, and their elements ooze and spill from the bread so readily, that although they still resemble sandwiches to a small degree, they cannot be eaten in any normal way. Even the application of knife and fork is sure to upset the balance, ultimately making for a

89

plate on which all the different ingredients, including the bread, have become a royal hodgepodge. It is common when ordering such sandwiches to request two or four extra slices of bread, then reapportion the ingredients in such a way that you have several hefty sandwiches made from all the stuff that composed the one. [20]

These are collations in which the enthusiasm for the sandwich becomes so great that it threatens to lose its status as sandwich. Elaboration can go too far.

The sandwich has also been a great vehicle for the expression of American individualism and choice. In 1906 May E. Southworth offered *One Hundred and One Sandwiches*, a number soon dwarfed by Eva Greene Fuller who wrote *The Up-to-Date Sandwich Book, 400 Ways to Make a Sandwich* (1909), revised in 1927 to '555 ways'. But even this figure was puny compared to Florence A. Cowles's *Seven Hundred Sandwiches* (1928) and her *1001 Sandwiches* of 1936: almost enough sandwiches to eat a different one every day for three whole years. In post-war Britain, sandwich fillings became relatively fixed and limited: cheese and pickle, egg and cress, ham and mustard. In America, the sky was the limit. A sandwich could contain anything your heart desired. In Florence Cowles's 1928 book, the peanut sandwiches alone cater for every imaginable taste as well as some unimaginable ones such as peanut butter and cabbage, peanut butter, cheese and olive and 'peanutpine' (peanut butter, honey, walnuts, lettuce and pineapple).

In Britain, pre-prepared sandwiches have remained the norm – the sand-wedges of Pret and Marks & Spencer come the way they come, all condiments and flavourings pre-chosen for you: like it or lump it. By contrast, the American deli sandwich caters for every whim of man, woman or child. You can have your tuna sandwich on white, wheat or rye; with

A branch of Subway in Cairo, showing how far the American sandwich has travelled.

pickles or without; with whatever salad you choose. Sandwiches in America are not necessarily fast food: in a good deli, you may need to wait ten minutes or so for your order to be made up, something which would have offended the impatient fourth earl.

But the American model of sandwich making is clearly one with global appeal.

The Subway chain of franchises, where the customer can 'alter' the basic formula of subs 'by choosing different vegetables, condiments and breads' now has more than 30,000 branches in 90 different countries. By choosing to have your sandwich with iceberg but not red onion or with honey mustard sauce instead of oil and vinegar or with sliced turkey instead of pastrami, you feel you are the architect of your own lunch. It makes a basic assemblage of meat and bread feel special; in a word, you are free to 'elaborate' as you choose.

5
The Global Sandwich

If you eat it and it reminds you of home, that is enough.

Thao Nguyen, a Vietnamese sandwich maker, quoted in
The New York Times (7 April 2009)

Right now, one of the most popular sandwiches in New
York City is Bánh mì: grilled pork and pâté stuffed into a
crusty baguette with lightly pickled vegetables (carrots and
daikon radish), coriander and perhaps some green chillies for
added fire. (Mayonnaise is optional.) Like all great sandwiches,
Bánh mì (pronounced bun mee) has immaculate balance: the
sour freshness of the vegetables and herbs offset the richness
of the pork. Any suspicion of dryness is warded off by the
pâté. It is a true global concoction, illustrating how a sandwich may be assembled from many disparate cultures and
countries yet retain its own delicious integrity.

Bread is not originally a Vietnamese food. The bread in
Bánh mì – baguette – was brought by the French to Indochina
in the early twentieth century, though the Saigon baguette was
different from its Parisian counterpart, being made with half
rice flour, half wheat flour, producing a lighter loaf. At first
these baguettes were eaten mainly by the French occupiers,
and might have contained little more than a smear of pâté, or

a restrained Gallic helping of ham and butter. But sometime around the 1940s, Vietnamese 'wannabes' craved the status of eating these sandwiches. One Vietnamese diner recalls how 'cheaper versions' of these French sandwiches started to show up in Vietnamese shops, usually including a coating of mayonnaise and some raw spring onion (scallion).[1] The sandwiches were labelled 'Bánh mì Tay', literally French bread. They started to be sold through mobile sandwich shops and included cheap but vibrant fillings such as green pepper, cucumber, pickles and herbs. The sandwich was eaten in Cambodia, too.

In 1954 the French finally left Indochina: the Geneva Conference recognized the territorial independence of Vietnam. But the 'Bánh mì Tay' remained a beloved snack. After the end of the Vietnam War in 1975, there was a wave of Vietnamese immigration to the States, followed by a second wave in 1978. The Vietnamese took their idea of a sandwich with them, but it took a new form when it met the overstuffed

Bánh mì: the Vietnamese sandwich that is conquering the rest of the world.

American deli sandwich. To start with, the immigrants couldn't buy Bánh mì, so they made their own. Julie Luong of Houston told *The New York Times*: 'When I was in college in New Orleans, the Vietnamese kids would buy a po'boy baguette, pull out the inside, put on liverwurst and Creole sausage and Miracle Whip. We all had pickles that our mothers sent us, and that was our Bánh mì.'[2]

By the new millennium, however, Bánh mì was a sufficiently well-established food in American cities that it started to come in new cultural variants. In the Polish district of New York, Bánh mì is made using Polish *kielbasa* in place of the traditional *cha lua* (pork terrine). At Baoguette, also in New York, they serve Sloppy Bao, a Bánh mì version of an American Sloppy Joe but made with fiery minced pork curry instead of ground beef. A food blog written from Vietnam lists some bizarre hybrids including Bánh mì bratwurst and Bánh mì doner kebab. In 2009 authentic Bánh mì arrived in London, at a tiny stall on Broadway Market called Banhmill; here you can eat a 'limited edition' version made from 'British rumpsteak' flavoured with soy and saké.[3]

In Philadelphia, city of the hoagie, Bánh mì is sold simply as 'Vietnamese Hoagie'. In 2009 I bought two Vietnamese hoagies from a Vietnamese grocery store in west Philadelphia, one filled with cold cuts along with the pickled vegetables and a vegetarian version with marinated tofu. 'These are Bánh mì, right?' I asked the young woman behind the counter, who was second-generation Vietnamese-American. 'Well, yes,' she replied, 'but when people come in and ask me for Bánh mì, I just laugh and say: these are all Bánh mì. Tuna hoagies are Bánh mì. Turkey hoagies are Bánh mì. It just means sandwich.'

What means 'sandwich' varies dramatically depending on where you are. If you are in Greece it might mean gyros in warm pitta with tzatziki, tomato and onion on top; in

Brazilian sandwich as served at Café Brazil, in Cambridge, England: chicken, olives, peppers and mayonnaise on a baguette.

Portugal, it could be a *Francesinha* (meaning Frenchie), a strange kind of croque monsieur invented in the 1960s made from ham and linguiça sausage, smothered in melted cheese and beer sauce; in Uruguay, it may be a *chivito* of steak, bacon, mayonnaise and olives in a crusty roll; in Finland, it could be a *porilainen*, a sausage sandwich made with gherkins; in New Zealand, it might be a cheddar sandwich stained with purple beetroot; and in the Dominican Republic, a sandwich may well be *chimmichurris*, roast pork and cabbage in a crusty roll.

To iterate the sandwich preferences of every country in the world would be a wearying and endless exercise. It is enough to say that no country seems entirely immune to the charms of the sandwich, partly because the form is so adaptable: you can change the bread, or the filling, or both.

There remains the mystery, however, of those nations that have stubbornly kept their sandwiches open-faced. Why does a Russian mother feel no compulsion to add a top slice when she makes a meal of bread, butter and smoked fish for her children? Throughout the countries of the Baltic and Scandinavia, it is normal for sandwiches to be open: Russian *zakuski* and *butterbrod*, Swedish *smörgås*, Norwegian *smorbrod* and Danish *smørrebrød*. In Denmark, *smørrebrød* is the single most important element of the cuisine. The majority of the restaurants in Copenhagen serve *smørrebrød*, slices of dense, dark rye bread artfully topped with any number of decorative fillings: eel, smoked salmon, herring, caviar, prawns, cucumber; but no second slice. What explains this attachment to half-finished sandwiches? All of these northern nations have a strong tradition of cold cuts and other delicatessen goodies: rollmops and other cured herring, smoked Baltic fish, pickles, cheeses, cured meats. In Denmark, there is a special word for this entire category of bread-toppers: *pålaeg*, which literally means 'that which is laid on'. With such riches to hand, it must have only seemed natural to display it, as in the classic Swedish smörgåsbord (whereas the true sandwich, as we have seen, was traditionally a more opportunistic and less considered meal, a bundling together of whatever ingredients were to hand).

Several other factors might have influenced the Baltic love of the open-faced sandwich. Firstly, all of these nations have a firm attachment to dark, wholesome bread. You might expect that serving sandwiches open reflects a desire not to eat too much bread, but the opposite seems to be true. In a genuine sandwich, the bread is subservient to the filling. In the very first reference to a sandwich in 1762, Gibbon called it 'a bit of cold meat, or a sandwich', the suggestion being that the meat is the important part. In a *butterbrod* or a *smørrebrød*, the bedrock is the *brød* – the bread. The Scandinavians and Russians love their bread so much that they choose to crown it with the most delicious items in their larder. Another factor may be that these countries have remained outside the orbit of the British Empire; during the nineteenth century the British were taking their sandwiches wherever their empire stretched, from India to Canada to Australia, as well as to America, which though politically separate still sat in Britain's cultural shadow. But Scandinavia and Russia remained apart: they did not look to Britain for tips on how to eat bread. A third reason is that, in contrast to the workaholic Anglo-Saxons, the Baltic countries retained some sense of ceremony to lunch. A classic *smørrebrød* lunch in Denmark might follow a three-course structure: first a herring one, then a cheese one, then meat; the fourth earl would have had no time for this. Russian mothers are partly able to make *butterbrod*, which do not travel well, for their children because the school day in Russia generally ends around one, meaning that children can come home to eat (unlike British children who get a hasty ham sandwich in a lunchbox to see them through till half past three).

Open sandwiches are fundamentally less transportable than real sandwiches: all those carefully positioned whirls of cucumber and lemon slices do not take kindly to being jiggled around in a lunchbox. Norway has got around this problem with the invention of *Mellomleggspapir*, or 'in-between paper', layers of which are placed over simplified open sandwiches (with toppings such as ham, cheese or liver pâté) when they are to be eaten outside the home. The whole package is then wrapped in *matpapir* (sandwich paper) to make a *matpakke* (sandwich lunch). At lunchtime, the parcel is unfolded and the *matpapir* is used as a makeshift plate. This is ingenious. But what a lot of trouble could be saved simply by adding another slice of bread!

The Baltic resistance to two-slice sandwiches is shifting, with globalization. There are now numerous chains in Moscow and St Petersburg selling Western-style sandwiches (including 'Prime', said to be very similar to the British Pret A Manger, complete with sand-wedges and wraps). With an ever-shrinking lunch hour, the Danes, too, have discovered that their cold cuts are every bit as delicious stuffed inside a couple of slices of rye bread or a halved baguette as when served as an elaborate *smørrebrød*. The true Anglo-Saxon sandwich continues its onward march.

Even France, which for a long time was said to be a nation highly suspicious of sandwich eaters, has succumbed to 'le sandwich'. The word 'sandwich' has been known in France since as early as 1830, when Lord Byron's French translator wrote a note saying that 'sandwiches' had started to be served at French dances, adding 'it's a slice of ham, or salted tongue, between two slices of bread with butter'.[4] However, sandwiches did not initially become a foundation of the national diet in France, as they did in Britain. Jean Camous, a great French chef, used to say that 'a Frenchman should not eat a sandwich. That is an English invention and horrible.' In 1984 Gwen Robyns could write, 'The French bourgeoisie have never taken to sandwiches. They simply do not know what to do with them and much prefer to use their bread to scoop up the sauce on their plate or dunk into the remains of the omelette.'[5] Fast forward to 2008, however, and the French were eating 1.3 billion sandwiches a year. Between 2003 and 2008 in France, wrote *The Economist*, 'the sandwich market jumped 28% in volume', pushed by a move to more Anglo-Saxon working hours and a decline in the long, leisurely lunch.[6] The upmarket sandwich chain Lina's sold itself with the slogan 'le beautiful sandwich'.

At least France has always had a deep tradition of eating bread. More striking are the examples of the rice-eating nations of Asia, which have adopted sandwiches despite no

A sign in Philadelphia advertising falafel sandwiches: another example of sandwich globalization.

prior attachment to bread. Both Korea and Japan are countries that traditionally got all of their carbohydrate from rice and various noodles. Yet from the mid-twentieth century onwards, both developed a significant culture of eating sandwiches made from white, sliced, processed, Western-style bread. In Korea the sandwiches are typically toasted and contain sweet omelette, as well as other fillings such as cabbage, bacon or *kimchi*, the nationally revered and very pungent pickle. There are a number of toasted sandwich franchises in Seoul: Isaac Toast, Toastoa, Sukbong Toast. In Japan, sandwiches or 'sandos' are typically untoasted and cold, with mayonnaise-heavy fillings: egg mayo, tuna mayo and so on. The crusts are cut off, in emulation of English afternoon tea. For children's lunchboxes or bentos, kitsch moulded sandwiches are some-times made in the shape of cute little animals.

Both Korean and Japanese sandwiches have come under criticism from those who complain that the sandwich has not adapted well in these cuisines. '[Has] anyone seen a Korean sandwich that doesn't look like it was assembled by a five-year-old let loose in the kitchen?' asks one food blog, complaining of a Korean recipe for a toasted white sandwich filled with breakfast cereal.[7] The typical convenience food, white-bread Japanese sandwich is said to be anaemic, with 'white, white, near non-nutritional value bread', filling that doesn't 'cover the sando' and English-language phrases on the wrapping, such as 'We hope this sando will bring you happy time'.[8]

On the other hand, Japan has a resurgent tradition of bread-baking. The Japanese *pan-yas*, or bakeries, serve an extra-ordinary range of sandwiches, with fillings from spaghetti to curry. In 1999 the Yonekura brothers were running a small Tokyo bakery serving an eclectic assortment of sandwiches. In the words of one visitor:

> Most Japanese sandwiches are actually rolls or buns with the filling baked in them. As well as spaghetti sandwiches, [the Yonekura brothers] make corn sandwiches, mashed potato sandwiches, mashed potato and corn sandwiches – for the adventurous, perhaps – green salad sandwiches, curry sandwiches and anko sandwiches, which use sweetened bean paste. Lately they have also been experi-menting very successfully with more Western types of sandwiches and in anticipation of the lunch rush, make piles of hamburgers, beef teriyaki sandwiches, tuna salad and their latest innovation, the kimchi beef sandwich, made with kimchi, a fiery Korean pickled cabbage.[9]

The bean sandwich referred to is *anpan*, in which sweet bean paste is baked as a filling inside bread. There is a popular cartoon on Japanese TV aimed at pre-school children starring Anpan-man, an unlikely superhero.

The Japanese enthusiasm for 'sandos' is not yet matched in China, where sandwich-eating is much more recent and reluctant. In America, numerous Chinese-style sandwiches are sold, ranging from chow-mein noodles squidged inside a hamburger bun to the Mantao Chinese sandwiches sold in New York City, which use as their bread a steamed bun similar to the 'lotus leaf buns' eaten in China. The Taiwanese, meanwhile, are fond of white bread sandwiches filled with Spam. In mainland China, though, sandwiches in the Western sense still seem somewhat alien. Fuchsia Dunlop, the leading Western expert on Chinese food, tells me that the Chinese 'don't really have this thing of slicing loaves of bread and then putting something between the slices'.[10] Subway opened its first branch in Beijing in 1995. Jim Bryant, the entrepreneur who brought Subway to China, discovered how resistant local customers were to the idea of sandwiches:

> They stood outside and watched for a few days, and when they finally tried to buy a sandwich, they were so confused that Bryant had to print signs explaining how to order a sandwich. They didn't believe the tuna salad was made from a fish, because they couldn't see the head or tail. And they didn't like the idea of touching their food, so they would hold the sandwich vertically, unpeel the paper wrap, and eat it like a banana. Most of all, his Chinese customers didn't want sandwiches.[11]

In the years since, Subway has opened more than a hundred branches in China – in Shanghai, Guangzhou and

Chengdu as well as Beijing. But China has not yet fully converted to American sandwiches. Stuffed flatbreads are another matter. In Sichuan they fill them with shredded vegetables and chilli sauce or cooked meat with its juices. In the northern region of Xi'an, they might be filled with stewed pork or lamb with cumin and called *jiamo*, 'jia' being a word which, as Fuchsia Dunlop explains, means 'to hold something between two other things, i.e. to sandwich'.[12] So China has its own concept of the sandwich after all.

Flatbread sandwiches are enjoyed in India, too, whether in the form of street kebabs or stuffed rotis, parathas, chapatis and nan. A sign of how much Indians like sandwiches is the existence of a product called 'Bombay magic sandwich masala', a spice mix specially devised to add 'tang' to sandwiches consisting of cumin, salt, black pepper, fennel, cinnamon, clove, mango powder and other spices. In a throwback to the days of the Raj – cucumber sandwiches on the terrace

An Indian Breville toasted curry sandwich.

– Indian sandwiches are often made with British-style sliced bread. In the nineteenth century Anglo-Indian fillings were made from such things as anchovies and sardines pounded with curry powder or egg and mango chutney. In 1930, in *Indian Curries, Soups and Sandwiches*, Cecelia Peel lists fairly dreary fillings – bloaters, game, potted meat, livened only with the occasional addition of chutney. Sweet Anglo-Indian sandwiches sound more appetizing: pineapple, for example, or stoned dates. Memsahibs were expected to carry sandwiches for a picnic in a large damp napkin, not a plantain leaf, which might affect the flavour of the bread.

Now, in these post-colonial times, the fillings are more likely to be entirely Indian. Various kinds of potato curry are popular, as is chana masala (chickpea curry). India has also taken the Breville sandwich maker to its heart, filling toasties with such delicacies as cabbage bhaji, chilli paneer or virtually any kind of dry vegetable curry, served with chutneys to dip the crisp edges of the sandwich into. But the Indian sandwich of sandwiches is probably the *vada pav*: a street food invented by a snack food vendor outside Dadar station in 1971. A deep-fried patty made from mashed potato (*batata vada*) is sandwiched in a bun (*pav*, from the Portuguese *pao*) with a coconut and tamarind chutney. Savoury, crisp and satisfying, it is India's answer to the hamburger.

Another great street sandwich is the choripán, which is Argentina's hotdog. The choripán – which is also eaten in Chile, Puerto Rico and Uruguay – consists of a blisteringly hot grilled chorizo sausage, wedged into a piece of baguette, usually with a drizzling of *chimichurri*, a herby and piquant sauce. The sausage can be served whole, hotdog style, or cut in half lengthwise like a butterfly – *mariposa*. Like the original English sandwich, the choripán serves both the worlds of work and play. In Buenos Aires, it is known as the food of cab

A choripán seller in Buenos Aires, Argentina.

drivers, who make a quick pit stop at choripán stalls between fares. But this spicy treat is also the food of football games, and is eaten at Peronist rallies, resulting in the political nickname 'choripaneros', or choripán-eaters, slang for someone vulgarly right wing. The nickname doesn't really work because practically everyone in Argentina, of whatever political persuasion, is a choripán-eater.

The choripán is a sandwich in the old, hearty, crusty tradition. There is another group of Argentine sandwiches, however, which are quite the opposite. Sandwiches *de miga* – white crustless sandwiches filled with ham and cheese, for example, or asparagus and mayonnaise, or cheese and salad – correspond to the old British afternoon tea sandwich. 'Miga' means the crumb of the bread. Sandwiches *de miga* are very similar to the tramezzini of Italy – soft little sandwiches with delicate fillings such as artichoke and ham, or tuna, olive and mayonnaise. Tramezzini are sold in many Italian bars throughout the day, or in the evening on a tray with a glass of white wine. They are often made with all the care an Edwardian cook would have brought to assembling a 5 o'clock tea, but they don't cost much and have no particular class connotation.

Tramezzini haven't travelled widely outside Italy. The same cannot be said for Panini, surely the most successful global sandwiches of modern times. If you were to split open a teenager almost anywhere on the globe at this moment, you would probably find that their insides had some Panini in them. These long hot sandwiches with dark grill lines down their length are now everywhere, from Starbucks to hospital canteens, from Paris to Johannesburg. No cafe worth its salt will be without a grooved Panini press, which flattens and cooks the sandwich at the same time.

Toasted Panini (panino just means little loaf) were first served in Italy's *panitecas* (sandwich shops) probably as long ago as the early 1900s. But it took the best part of the century for them to reach the rest of the world. In 1954 *The New York Times* referred to Italians eating 'zeppole, calzone, torrone, panini', as if such things were all deeply exotic. Young people in Italy came to be known as *paninari* – too busy to stop for anything but a quick Panini.

It would be the late 1980s before Panini became a household name in the world beyond Italy. In 1987 the *LA Times* wrote: 'I'll bet a hundred bucks that panino, the Italian word for sandwich, will soon slip off your tongue like honey.' That's a hundred dollars gone: the singular, panino, has never become well known in the English language. But Panini (invariably capitalized, and used interchangeably for singular and plural) has. And how. Panini – with their reassuring black bar stripes all down the bread – are now completely ubiquitous, and are another worldwide phenomenon. You can get Panini not just in Rome, Florence and Venice but in Riyadh,

An Italian sandwich stall selling a range of tramezzini and Panini.

Ham Sandwich road sign.

Mumbai and Jakarta. At the Soho Sandwich Company in north London, a globalized modern sandwich bar with an award-winning menu and a young feel, you can get the following Panini flavours: Cajun chicken; honey roast ham; French brie and smoked streaky bacon; Soho tuna melt; giant fish finger melt; chicken escalope melt with Swiss cheese and fresh tomato; Soho all day veggie breakfast (V); and roasted vegetable melt (V) with buffalo mozzarella and creamy basil pesto mayo. These Panini make no false attempt at being Italian; they do not belong to any particular nation or culture; the charred bread is just a useful vehicle for transporting different fillings to different people.

Like all sandwiches, Panini are best understood not as a particular dish – a fixed combination of specific ingredients – but as a way of eating. It has not for the most part been the most sociable way. Unlike family dinners or lazy lunches which bring us together over chat and food and perhaps some wine, sandwiches generally push us ever further into our isolated little bubbles. Sandwiches are a sober and selfish food. All over the world, people are choosing the sandwich which bests chimes with their particular diet or desires, then retreating to eat it by themselves, probably while staring at a screen. Sandwiches freed us from the fork, the dinner table, the fixed meal time. In a way, they freed us from society itself. We may lament this or we may welcome it, but there is not much point in fighting it. This is the way we eat now.

Recipes

Historical Sandwiches

To Make Oyster Loaves
—from Mary Randolph, *The Virginia HouseWife*, 1824

Take little round loaves, cut off the top, scrape out all the crumbs, then put the oysters into a stew pan with the crumbs that came out of the loaves, a little water and a good lump of butter; stew them together ten or fifteen minutes, then put in a spoonful of good cream, fill your loaves, lay a bit of crust carefully on again, set them in the oven to crisp. Three are enough for a side dish.

Sandwiches of Various Kinds, for Picnics
—from Lafcadio Hearn, *La Cuisine Creole*, New Orleans, *c.* 1885

Home-made bread cuts better for sandwiches than baker's bread, so if you wish the sandwiches very nice, it is better to make a loaf at home. For bread and butter sandwiches, cut the bread very thin, spread it evenly with sweet butter, and lay the buttered sides together. Lay them in circles on a plate and put parsley on top of them. Sandwiches may be made with cheese sliced and placed between the buttered bread, or with hard-boiled eggs sliced or chopped, and put between. The best are made with boiled smoked tongue or ham, with French mustard spread over the butter.

Victorian Lamb and Mint Sandwiches
—from T. Herbert, *Salads and Sandwiches*, 1890

Lamb, sliced, young leaves of mint and a squeeze of lemon.

Cheese Sandwiches
—from Isabel Gordon Curtis, *The Good Housekeeping Woman's Home Cook Book*, 1909

To half a cup of mild grated cheese and half a cup of Roquefort cheese rubbed to a paste, add one teaspoon of paprika and half a cup of cream. Beat till smooth and spread between graham bread.

A Double Sandwich
—from Mrs Leyel, *Savoury Cold Meals*, 1927

Slice radishes as thin as wafers; spread them between two lettuce leaves, and place this sandwich between another sandwich of bread and butter.

Dream Sandwiches
—from Florence Jack, *One Hundred Salads and Sandwiches*, 1928

Make small sandwiches of bread and cheese, trimming off all the crusts. Beat up an egg with a little milk, dip the sandwiches into this, without making them too pappy, then fry them in hot butter, browning on both sides.

Green Fig and Almond Sandwich
—from Mrs Leyel, *Savoury Cold Meals*, 1927

Crush the figs into a puree. Spread it on white bread and butter. Blanch some sweet almonds, chop them coarsely and put amongst the puree. Make it into a sandwich.

Russian Club Sandwich
—from Florence A Cowles, *Seven Hundred Sandwiches*, 1929

This is a miniature course dinner, beginning with fruit cocktail and ending with a sweet. Cut six thin, round slices of bread, the smallest an inch and a half in diameter and the largest four inches. Lay the largest slice on a plate and spread with jam. On it lay the next largest slice of bread and spread with cream cheese. Then the next slice, buttered, and on this lay bacon or chicken with lettuce and mayonnaise. On the fourth piece of bread lay a slice of tomato and on the fifth a slice of cucumber, each slice of bread being buttered and each vegetable having a bit of mayonnaise and lettuce. On the top piece of bread, unbuttered, lay a slice of banana or other fruit and crown with a stuffed olive. If the layers prove topply they may be secured with toothpicks, but avoid this if possible.

Asparagus Rolls
—from Cecilia Peel, *Indian Curries, Soups and Sandwiches*, 1930

Tinned asparagus of the white thick variety is the best to use for this sandwich. Drain the asparagus and cut it into pieces of the same length as the slices of bread. Cut the bread very thinly, spread sparsely with mayonnaise sauced, lay on the asparagus at one end and roll it up in the bread.

Buzz Bee Sandwiches

—from Arnold Shircliffe, *The Edgewater Sandwich Book*, 1975/1930

White bread, honey, lemon, butter.

Spread the lower thin slice of white bread with strained white clover honey, to which has been added a little lemon juice, and the upper slice with sweet butter. Lettuce and press together. Cut in fancy shapes and serve. Sandwiches may be garnished with small cubes of comb honey or small nests of cream cheese filled with honey or bar le duc. Honeysuckle, nasturtium or clover blossoms make an attractive garniture.

Golf Club

—from Shircliffe 1975/1930: a variant on the club sandwich

Toast, lettuce, turkey, tomato, green pepper, Thousand Island dressing, caviar.

'Atta-Boy!'

—from M. Redington White, *Something New in Sandwiches*, 1933

Cut the corn from the required number of green corn cobs and cook it in slightly salted water, stirring frequently. At the end of half-an-hour add milk, butter, salt and pepper and cook for ten more minutes, stirring all the time. The corn should now be thick and pulpy. Have ready three slices of hot buttered toast. Spread the lowest with hot minced bacon and a few very tender French beans, cooked and hot. Add second slice and spread with the corn. Cover with third slice and serve.

Nasturtium
—from Ambrose Heath, *Sandwiches and Picnic Dishes*, 1949

We are often counselled to use the chopped leaves of the nasturtium for a sandwich filling, but this recipe demands the flowers. Spread some bread with mayonnaise and lay the separate flower petals closely together on it. Then cover with a similar slice.

Egg Salad, Chopped Olives and Tomato-Anchovy-Lettuce on Toast
—from Louis P. de Gouy, *Sandwich Exotica*, 1975

LL Covered with EGG SALAD, topped with CHOPPED OLIVES.
SL Covered with TOMATO SLICES, then with ANCHOVY filets, and topped with lettuce leaves.
[NB: LL = lower layer of toast; SL = second layer of toast; the sandwich is finished, club-style, with a third layer of toast]

Modern Sandwiches

Martin's Sugar Sandwich
—from Bee Wilson, Hilary Cox and Ruth Platt, eds, *What's for Tea? Family Recipes from St Matthew's School*, 2007

Martin Smart writes, 'Most of the time I give the kids sensible food, but sometimes I like to surprise them with this silly treat. Butter a slice of bread. Sprinkle liberally with sugar. Fold over and press down.'

Indian Toasted Sandwich

Take a tablespoon or so of any reasonably dry leftover vegetable curry – the best is cauliflower and potato or spinach bhaji. Spread the cold curry on a slice of bread. Top with cubes of fried paneer (white Indian cheese), salt, pepper and perhaps some fresh chopped coriander/red chilli/spring onion. Top with a second slice of bread and toast for 3–4 minutes in a Breville toaster. Serve with chutneys for dipping.

'pbjs'
— As mentioned by Amanda Hesser, *Cooking for Mr Latte*, 2003

Hesser, who got the idea from Bernadette Cura, makes a grown-up version of 'PBJs' to serve as hors d'oeuvres: foie gras mousse (instead of peanut butter) and tart berry jam (instead of grape jelly) spread between slices of 'soft and buttery' white bread, cut into little quarters.

Tomato Sandwich

In some ways, this simple summer sandwich is a great luxury because it has to be made and eaten so fresh. You could never get a pre-made tomato 'sand-wedge' because the tomato juices would seep into the bread. Take some slices from a fresh white loaf. Butter liberally. Add slices of sweet ripe tomatoes – which must be at room temperature, not from the fridge – and season assertively with salt and pepper. Some might add a few basil leaves, or a sprinkling of celery salt before closing off with the second slice; it doesn't need them; it has a perfect Enid Blyton charm just as it is. For some reason, I think this is best sliced into two rectangles, instead of triangles.

A Good Beef Sandwich in honour of the Fourth Earl

Best made the day after you have cooked a roast beef dinner; any roast beef would do – topside or rib or, for the height of luxury, fillet or sirloin. Slice the cold roast beef thinly and pile between two slices of bread, which you have first spread on one side with unsalted butter, and on the other with fiery horseradish or sinus-clearing English mustard. Add a layer of watercress or sliced tomato, press together and eat in a great hurry.

Pâté and Pear

I remember this sandwich as the best ever. I ate one every day for a week, bought from a nearby sandwich shop, as a graduate student while doing research at the old Bibliothèque Nationale on the rue de Richelieu in Paris. The sandwich consisted of smooth chicken liver pâté with a sweet pear chutney on thin slices of *pain Poilâne*. It neither had, nor needed, any salad to punctuate the smoothness of the pâté and pear. It was soothing and nourishing just as it was. I knew no one in Paris. As I sat by myself eating my lunch in a courtyard opposite the library each day, I felt that my sandwich was keeping me company.

My Favourite Sandwich

Any savoury sandwich can be turned into a feast with the addition of some dark green leaves and a tart vinaigrette. This solves the problem of whether to have a salad or a sandwich: you get both in one satisfying mouthful. The vinaigrette serves both as lubricant – no need for butter – and condiment, leaving the sandwich perfectly seasoned. I am happy to make vinaigrette sandwiches out of anything left in the fridge. In its ideal form, however, it would go something like this. Make a vinaigrette shaken in a jam jar from 3 parts extra virgin olive oil to 1 part white wine vinegar, plus a large pinch each of sugar and Maldon sea salt. Take two thinnish slices of day-old sourdough (white or brown, doesn't matter) and lightly toast. Spread one slice with a mild goat's cheese and drape over a slice of Parma ham (other good fillings are: leftover roast chicken and bottled artichokes; Gruyère and sliced raw mushrooms; houmous, grated carrot and pumpkin seeds). Cram on as many green leaves as you can easily fit on top. Spoon over vinaigrette and press the second slice of toast on top. Cut in half any which way and eat. It can also be made with half a ciabatta sliced lengthwise instead of the toast. This makes an ideal solitary lunch if you work at home.

Appendix:
Fifty Notable Sandwiches

Bacon Sandwich (Bacon Sarnie)
COMPOSITION: Fried bacon (either back bacon or streaky bacon) in between two slices of bread or toast with tomato ketchup or brown sauce.
ORIGIN: a British breakfast dish; in Scotland it is known as 'piece 'n' bacon'.

Bánh Mì
COMPOSITION: Technically, this just means 'bread' in Vietnamese, but the sandwich generally known as Bành Mí outside Vietnam typically contains pâté, grilled pork or other meats, lightly pickled carrots and daikon radish, leaf coriander and chillies stuffed into a length of white baguette or **Hoagie**.
ORIGIN: Vietnam, but now served globally e.g. in New York, London, Sydney, Melbourne (in Australia, this sandwich is sometimes called a Vietnamese Lunch Roll).

Barros Luco (also Barros Jarpa)
COMPOSITION: Sandwich of steak and melted cheese, prepared on the grill, served hot. The **Barros Jarpa** is the same, but with ham instead of beef.
ORIGIN: Chile. Named after President Ramón Barros Luco, president of Chile from 1910–15 who often ate this particular sandwich at the National Congress in Santiago. The **Barros Jarpa** was named after another politician, Minister Ernesto Barros Jarpa.

Bauru

COMPOSITION: A combination of three cheeses melted in a double boiler (now often just mozzarella) with roast beef, tomato and gherkins in a French roll, some of whose crumb has been removed.

ORIGIN: First ordered by a customer (a radio host called Casemiro Pinto Neto who came from the town of Bauru) at the Ponto Chic café in São Paolo in 1934.

Beef on Weck

COMPOSITION: Rare roast beef and horseradish on a caraway-flecked kummelweck roll.

ORIGIN: Western New York and Western Pennsylvania.

Belegde Broodje

COMPOSITION: A cold sandwich made of crusty baguette-type bread filled with cold meats or cheese and other fillings.

ORIGIN: Netherlands. Some version of these sandwiches has been eaten for hundreds of years.

BLT

COMPOSITION: Bacon, lettuce, tomato and mayonnaise sandwiched between sliced bread or toast.

ORIGIN: USA, in its current form probably dates from diners of the 1930s, where such abbreviations were normal; earlier American bacon sandwich recipes feature lettuce but not tomato.

Bocadillo de Tortilla

COMPOSITION: A wedge of cold Spanish omelette (made from eggs, onions and potatoes) in a crusty piece of white bread.

ORIGIN: Traditional Spanish bar, canteen and street food; the first printed reference to *tortilla de patata* is 1817; the sandwich followed some time after.

Bun Kabab

COMPOSITION: Spicy lentil patty (or variants made with meat) in a hamburger bun or hotdog roll.

ORIGIN: Pakistan.

Caprese
COMPOSITION: Mozzarella, basil and tomato, sliced and interleaved in white crusty bread (perhaps ciabatta): a sandwich version of the salad of the same name.
ORIGIN: Capri, Italy.

Caviar Sandwich
COMPOSITION: Caviar (whether real sturgeon caviar or some substitute such as lumpfish roe), cream cheese or sour cream and grated onion, in rye bread.
ORIGIN: Eaten throughout Scandinavia and also in Russia and Eastern Europe.

Cheesesteak (aka Philly Cheesesteak)
COMPOSITION: Thin slices of beef cooked with onions and topped with processed cheese (either Kraft slices or Cheez Whiz from an aerosol can) and other condiments in a crisp Italian roll or **Hoagie**.
ORIGIN: Philadelphia (possibly first served at Pat's King O'Steaks in 1930).

Chimichurris
COMPOSITION: A spit-roasted pork sandwich, often garnished with cabbage. Sometimes described as the 'Dominican hamburger'.
ORIGIN: Dominican republic in the Caribbean, where it is often sold from trucks.

Chip Butty (aka French Fry Sandwich)
COMPOSITION: Chips (French fries) in buttered white bread (or a bap – 'chip bap') doused with either ketchup or brown sauce. Kebab shop variant: chips in pitta bread with mayonnaise.
ORIGIN: UK, sold in chip shops especially in the North of England.

Chivito

COMPOSITION: Churrasco beef, olives, mozzarella, tomatoes, bacon, perhaps with the addition of sweet peppers or pickles served in a bun, usually with French fries.

ORIGIN: The national sandwich of Uruguay; chivito means 'little goat'; it has been suggested that the word got attached to the sandwich when a customer from Argentina ordered baby goat at a restaurant in Punta del Este; she was served this instead.

Christmas Sandwich (also Chicken and Stuffing)

COMPOSITION: Leftover roast turkey, stuffing, cranberry sauce etc.

ORIGIN: Eaten in the UK and USA, exact origin not known; a 'Christmas week' sandwich of roast turkey, mashed potato and chestnut sauce was published in 1933.

Choripán

COMPOSITION: Grilled chorizo sausage inside a crisp white baguette-type roll, sometimes with herby chimichurri sauce.

ORIGIN: Argentina, Uruguay, Chile.

Club Sandwich

COMPOSITION: Chicken, bacon, lettuce, tomato, mayonnaise, usually sandwiched between toasted bread, either two or three slices, held together with cocktail sticks. Sometimes used just to refer to any double-decker sandwich.

ORIGIN: USA, late nineteenth century.

Cream Cheese with Lox
(aka Smoked Salmon and Cream Cheese)

COMPOSITION: Cream cheese and smoked salmon, served either inside a bagel or between two slices of rye or wholemeal bread, sometimes with the addition of capers; in England, smoked salmon sandwiches are traditionally made with butter rather than cream cheese.

ORIGIN: USA, Jewish-American deli food.

Croque-Monsieur

COMPOSITION: Hot ham and cheese sandwich made from white bread (or soft *pain de miè*), with a layer of béchamel sauce (preferably seasoned with nutmeg). The cheese should be Gruyère or emmenthal; the ham should be thin and cooked. Many variants include **Croque-Madame** (with a fried egg); **Croque-Señor** (with salsa); **Croque-Provençal** (with tomato); **Croque-Auvergnat** (with bleu d'Auvergne cheese); **Croque-Hawaiian** (with pineapple); **Croque-Norvégien** (with smoked salmon); and **Croque McDo** from McDonald's, which is circular like a hamburger.

ORIGIN: A French snack-bar food, origins unclear but it dates from the early twentieth century. The name comes from croquer (to crunch) and Monsieur (sir).

Cucumber Sandwiches

COMPOSITION: Very thinly sliced cucumber on very thinly sliced white buttered bread, crusts off, cut into triangles.

ORIGIN: An English afternoon tea food, nineteenth century.

Dagwood

COMPOSITION: As many incongruent ingredients as possible, all piled into a tower between multiple slices of bread.

Origin: USA, first invented in the *Blondie* comic strip in 1936.

Egg and Cress

COMPOSITION: Chopped hard-boiled eggs, mayonnaise, salad cress, all sandwiched between bread, often from a malted granary loaf.

ORIGIN: Traditional English.

Elvis Sandwich

COMPOSITION: A white sliced bread sandwich of peanut butter and mashed banana, sometimes with added bacon, fried until golden in butter or bacon fat.

ORIGIN: USA, as eaten by Elvis Presley (1935–1977).

Falafel Sandwich

COMPOSITION: Fried spiced chickpea patties, wrapped in flatbread or stuffed in pitta with tahini sauce or houmous salad, and sometimes pickles and hot sauce.

ORIGIN: Probably originated in Egypt many centuries ago, now eaten all over the Arab world and beyond. In western Europe, it is a popular food among vegans; falafel stalls are a regular fixture at pop concerts.

Fish Finger Sandwich

COMPOSITION: Fish fingers (breaded fish sticks), white bread, tartare sauce.

ORIGIN: British folk food, origins unknown, often made at home.

Fluffernutter

COMPOSITION: A variant of the PBJ but made with 'marshmallow fluff' from a jar instead of jam.

ORIGIN: New England, USA.

Francesinha

COMPOSITION: A kind of wet **croque-monsieur**, made from a sandwich of ham, linguiça sausage and other meats covered in melted cheese with a thick beer-based sauce poured over the top.

ORIGIN: Porto, Portugal, probably originated in the 1960s.

Gyros (Doner Kebab, Shawarma, etc.)

COMPOSITION: Ground lamb cooked on a vertical spit, stuffed into pitta bread with onions, tomatoes, shredded lettuce, hot sauce, etc. Also, **Souvlaki**: grilled chunks of lamb treated similarly.

ORIGIN: Some version of the grilled lamb-in-flatbread sandwich has been eaten in the Middle East since ancient times.

Hoagie (aka Grinder, Hero, Sub, Wedge, etc.)

COMPOSITION: A soft Italian loaf sliced lengthwise and filled with a variety of cold meats and salad vegetables, and dressed with oil and vinegar; also hot variations such as the **meatball sub** (containing hot meatballs in tomato sauce) and the **veal parmigiana**

hero (breaded veal cutlet, mozzarella cheese, tomato sauce). ORIGIN: USA, east coast, Italian-American.

Lampredotto

COMPOSITION: Boiled tripe from the fourth and final stomach of the cow, served in a crusty roll with green *salsa verde* and spicy red *salsa piccante*; the roll may be served *bagnato*, i.e. bathed in the meat juices.

ORIGIN: Served from stalls all over Florence, Italy, by *lampredottai*; there have been tripe sellers in Florence since the 1400s.

Lobster Roll

COMPOSITION: Cooked lobster meat, chopped celery and green onion mixed with mayonnaise and piled into a hotdog bun.

ORIGIN: Invented by Harry Perry of Milford, Connecticut in 1929 at his seafood shack; originally made using butter instead of mayonnaise and served hot. Now eaten all over New England; a famously good version is also served at Pearl Oyster Bay, New York City (www.pearloysterbar.com).

Mantao Chinese Sandwiches

COMPOSITION: Various fillings (including spicy pork and sliced beef) inside steamed Chinese sesame-seed-topped bread.

ORIGIN: Mantao Chinese sandwiches began being served in New York City in 2009; but something similar, heyebing or 'lotus leaf buns' have been wrapped around roast pork and other fillings for many years in China.

Marmite Sandwich (also Vegemite Sandwich)

COMPOSITION: Marmite yeast extract and butter spread inside two pieces of sliced bread; the Marmite can be spread on top of the butter or, in Nigella Lawson's version, can be beaten into the butter to make a buff-coloured Marmite sandwich filling.

ORIGIN: British (Marmite dates from 1902), frequently made for children's packed lunches and parties. Vegemite sandwiches are the Australian equivalent; Vegemite was first marketed in 1922.

Melts (Tuna Melt, Patty Melt, Turkey Melt, etc.)

COMPOSITION: A toasted sandwich filled with some kind of filling – tuna, turkey, meat patty, etc. – with a layer of melted cheese.
ORIGIN: USA, twentieth-century diner food.

Monte Cristo

COMPOSITION: An American version of the French Croque-Monsieur, a sandwich classically consisting of ham, chicken and Swiss cheese in white bread, dipped in beaten egg and fried.
ORIGIN: USA 1930s, also known as 'French sandwich'.

Muffaletta

COMPOSITION: A large round flat loaf, approximately 10 inches (25 cm) in diameter, hollowed out and filled with many layers of olive salad (olives, cauliflower, celery, carrots, oil, vinegar), cured meats (salami, mortadella, capicola) and cheese (emmentaler, provolone), wrapped in wax paper; to serve, the entire sandwich is cut into hunks; one sandwich feeds several people.
ORIGIN: New Orleans, 1906, first made by Salvatore Lupo from Sicily at the Central Grocery.

Panini (Panino)

COMPOSITION: Toasted sandwiches made from long white bread, split horizontally and filled, e.g. with mozzarella and ham, before being toasted on a special Panini press, which gives the bread distinctive 'bar' markings.
ORIGIN: Italian, probably at least a hundred years old; but popularized through the Milanese *paninoteche* of the 1970s; and now a global food, eaten and recognized almost everywhere.

Pastrami on Rye

COMPOSITION: Pastrami (cured brisket) piled up between rye bread; cucumber pickles are often served on the side.
ORIGIN: A Jewish-American food; probably dates to the mid nineteenth century; now associated with Jewish delis, e.g. Katz's in New York (www.katzdeli.com).

Peanut Butter and Jelly (aka PBJ)

COMPOSITION: A layer of peanut butter and a layer of jam/jelly (classically grape flavour but strawberry is also permissible) on white sandwich bread. A variant is the CJ (cream cheese and jelly). See also **Fluffernutter.**

ORIGIN: USA.

Po'Boy

COMPOSITION: A crusty sandwich from Louisiana, often containing fried seafood such as shrimp, crab or oysters, though po'boys can also be made from sausage or roast beef or even French fries dressed with a gravy called debris.

ORIGIN: USA; the po'boy probably dates from New Orleans in the 1920s, when they were served at the Martin Brothers grocery, though Mariani states that 'the term "poor boy" for a sandwich goes back to 1875' and a recipe for **Oyster Loaves**, a variant of the po'boy (a crusty loaf filled with cooked oysters) can be dated to 1824 (in Mary Randolph's *The Virginia Housewife*). There is disagreement about the etymology of po'boy: Becky Mercuri suggests it may come from 'hungry young black boys requesting a sandwich "for a po'boy"' while Mariani notes that the term could derive from the French pourboire, meaning a tip.

Porchetta Sandwich

COMPOSITION: Pork (properly, it should be suckling pig) marinated and roasted with rosemary, garlic, fennel seeds and sage, used to fill a dry crusty white roll.

ORIGIN: Served all over Italy, especially in the Lazio region; it has been adapted by Italian immigrants to the USA., e.g. in the Italian roast pork sandwich served at Tony Luke's, Philadelphia, where the pork is combined with sautéed broccoli rabe (a kind of bitter greens); also very popular in Canada.

Porilainen

COMPOSITION: Sausage, onion, pickled cucumber, ketchup, in toast. Origin: Finland, where it is eaten as a fast food.

Reuben

COMPOSITION: Corned beef (the American kind, not the British canned variety), sauerkraut, Swiss cheese and Russian dressing on rye bread; sometimes coleslaw is substituted for the sauerkraut.

ORIGIN: USA, 1920s, though the exact moment of invention is contested. A classic diner/deli food.

Sandwiches de Miga

COMPOSITION: crustless white sandwiches, similar to Italian **Tramezzini**, filled with thin ham, eggs, salad, mayonnaise, etc.

ORIGIN: Argentina.

Sloppy Joe

COMPOSITION: Ground beef, onions, green peppers and ketchup, all cooked together and served freeform in a hamburger roll.

ORIGIN: USA, 1930s (first printed reference 1935); also known as a **Loosemeat sandwich**, and a **Manwich**, a brand of Sloppy Joe sauce first sold in 1969; slogan: 'A sandwich is a sandwich but a Manwich is a meal'.

Toasties (Brevilles, Jaffles etc.)

COMPOSITION: Any filling imaginable (from cheese and pickles to banana and Nutella) sandwiched and toasted between two slices of bread.

ORIGIN: Sandwiches fashioned from toast have been made at least since the eighteenth century, but the Breville 'Snack 'n' Sandwich Maker' with its distinctive 'Cut 'n' Seal' mechanism was only launched in 1974. In South Africa and Australia, toasted sandwiches are called **Jaffles**. See also **Panini, Melts, Croque-Monsieur, Monte Cristo.**

Tramezzini

COMPOSITION: Crustless white sandwiches based on English afternoon tea sandwiches, filled with such things as bottled artichokes, ham, mayonnaise, olives, tuna.

ORIGIN: Italy; said to be invented at Caffè Mulassano di Piazza Castello in Turin; also popular in Venice.

Western Sandwiches (aka Denver Sandwiches)

COMPOSITION: Scrambled eggs or omelette flavoured with ham, green peppers and onions, inside a roll or toast.

ORIGIN: The American West; the term 'western omelette' first appeared in print in 1935; 'Denver sandwich' first appeared in print in 1918.

Vada Pav

COMPOSITION: Deep-fried spiced mashed potato patties in a bun (*pav*).

ORIGIN: India, 1971, first devised by street vendor Ashok Vaidya outside Dadar railway station, Mumbai.

References

Introduction

1 Andrew F. Smith, 'Sandwiches', *The Oxford Encyclopaedia of Food and Drink in America* (Oxford, 2004), p. 399.
2 'Sandwich Facts and Figures to Make Your Mouth Water', at www.sandwich.org.uk (accessed November 2009).
3 Isabella Beeton, *The Book of Household Management* (London, 1860) recipe 1877.
4 Jenn Abelson, 'Arguments Spread Thick: Rivals Aren't Serving Same Food, Judge Rules', *The Boston Globe* (10 November 2006).

1 The History of the Sandwich: The Fourth Earl and What Came Before

1 *Larousse Gastronomique* (London, 2001) p. 1038.
2 Charles Lamb refers to this epigram in a letter dated 20 January 1825 to Sarah Hutchinson.
3 Woody Allen, *Getting Even* (New York, 1971).
4 Alan Davidson, 'Le sandwich d'un joueur', in *Le Dossier: Casse-Croute: aliment portative, repas indéfinissale*, ed. Julia Csergo (Paris, 2001).
5 N.A.M. Rodger, *The Insatiable Earl: A Life of John Montagu, Fourth Earl of Sandwich (1718–1792)* (London, 1993), p. 79.

6 Ibid., p. 79.

7 Ibid., p. 319.

8 Conversation with the author (July 2009).

9 Charlotte Mason, *The Lady's assistant for regulating and supplying her table; containing one hundred and fifty select bills of fare* (1773), p. 125.

10 Philip B. Dodd, *The Reverend Guppy's Aquarium: Encounters with the Heroes of the English Language* (London, 2007), pp. 166–7.

11 Ibid., p. 159; www.earlofsandwichusa.com, accessed April 2010.

12 Interview with the author (July 2009).

13 Dodd, *Reverend Guppy*, p. 165.

14 Charles Panati, *Panati's Extraordinary Origins of Everyday Things* (New York, 1987), p. 400.

15 Gwen Robyns, *The Book of Sandwiches* (London and Sydney, 1984), p. 10.

16 Hugh Rhodes, *The Boke of Nurtur for Men Servants* (London, 1560).

17 Susan Weingarten, 'Haroset' in *Authenticity in the Kitchen: Proceedings on the Oxford Symposium on Food and Cookery 2005* (Totnes, 2006), p. 414.

18 C. Anne Wilson, *Food and Drink in Britain: From the Stone Age to Recent Times* (London, 1973), p. 265.

19 Eliza Leslie, *The Lady's Receipt-Book* (Philadelphia, 1847), p. 29.

20 Mark Morton, 'Bread and Meat for God's Sake', *Gastronomica* (Summer 2004), p. 6.

21 John Northbrooke, *Spiritus est vicarious Christi in terra* (London, 1571).

22 John Ray, *Observations Topographical, Moral and Physiological made in a Journey through part of the Low-Countries* (London, 1673), p. 51.

23 Simon Schama, *The Embarrassment of Riches* (London, 1987), p. 157.

24 For reproductions of these pictures see Donna R. Barnes and Peter G. Rose, *Matters of Taste: Food and Drink in Seventeenth-Century Dutch Art and Life* (Albany, NY, 2002).

25 Charles Dickens, *The Old Curiosity Shop* (London, 1840), vol.
1, chapter 1.

2 Constructing the Sandwich

1 C. Anne Wilson, *Food and Drink in Britain: From the Stone Age to Recent Times* (London, 1973), p. 265.

2 Joseph Pearson, *Pearson's Political Dictionary* (London, 1793), 'S'.

3 *Morning Post and Daily Advertiser* (6 September 1788); *The Times* (5 June 1789).

4 *The Times* (3 December 1796).

5 T. Herbert, *Salads and Sandwiches* (London, 1890), p. 21.

6 Arabella Boxer, *Arabella Boxer's Book of English Food* (London, 1993).

7 Quoted in Alan Davidson, 'Le sandwich d'un joueur', in *Le Dossier: Casse-Croute: aliment portative, repas indéfinissale*, ed. Julia Csergo (Paris, 2001).

8 Quoted in ibid.

9 Henry Mayhew, *London Labour and the London Poor* (London, 1851), vol. 1, chapter 9, 'Of the Experience of a Ham Sandwich Seller'.

10 Mayhew, *London Labour*, vol. 1, p. 178.

11 Letter to *The Times* from J. R. Williams (10 September 1948).

12 Robert Uhlig, 'Recycled Sandwiches Put Back on the Shelf', *Daily Telegraph* (24 January 2003).

13 Joe Moran, *Queuing for Beginners: The Story of Daily Life from Breakfast to Bedtime* (London, 2007), p. 75.

14 Nigel Bunyan, 'Revealed: The Secrets of a British Rail Sandwich', *Daily Telegraph* (22 November 2002).

15 Moran, *Queuing*, p. 79; Judi Bevan, *The Rise and Fall of Marks and Spencer: And How it Rose Again* (London, 2007).

16 U. D. Parasher, L. Dow, R. L. Fankhauser et al., 'An Outbreak of Viral Gastroenteritis Associated with the Consumption of Sandwiches: Implications for the Control

of Transmission by Food Handlers', *Epidemiology and Infection*, CXXI/3 (December 1998), p. 620.

17 R. J. Meldrum, R.M.M. Smith et al., 'Microbiological Quality of Randomly Selected Ready-to-eat Foods Sampled Between 2003 and 2005 in Wales, UK', *International Journal of Food Microbiology*, CVIII (2006), p. 400.

18 'Sandwiches that Serve up as Much Salt as 18 Packets of Crisps', *Daily Mail* (25 July 2008).

19 Sally Parsonage, 'How to Choose Your Slice of Life', *The Times* (9 May 1975).

20 'The Household Column', *Manchester Times* (18 January 1890).

21 Kevin Reed, 'Old Lunch Boxes Now Pack Memories, Big Bucks for Collectors', *Pop Culture* (25 August 2000).

22 Marrion Burros, 'Presses New and Old Prove that Panini Aren't Picky', *New York Times* (17 July 2002).

23 Classified section, *The Caledonian Mercury* (20 October 1851).

24 Bee Wilson, 'Enzymes', *The Food Magazine*, 86 (2009).

25 M. Redington White, *Something New in Sandwiches* (London, 1933), pp. ix, 78–80.

26 Tristram Stuart, *Waste: Uncovering the Global Food Scandal* (London, 2009), p. 45.

27 Stephen Miller, *Starting and Running a Sandwich-Coffee Bar* (London, 2002) pp. 98–9.

28 *The Guardian*, word of mouth blog, 7 April 2010.

3 Who Eats Sandwiches?

1 'Observer of the Times', *A Diary of the Royal Tour in June, July, August and September 1789* (1789), p. 97.

2 *European Magazine*, LXIV (1813), p. 336.

3 Charlotte Mason, *The Lady's assistant for regulating and supplying her table; containing one hundred and fifty select bills of fare* (1773), p. 125.

4 Henry James Pye, *Sketches on Various Subjects* (1797), p. 176.

5 *Louisa Matthews* by an eminent lady (1793).

6 *The Times* (26 February 1802).

7 Charles Dickens, *Little Dorrit* (1857), book 2, chapter 9.

8 Letter to *The Times* (23 September 1883).

9 Letter to *The Times* (5 February 1918).

10 *The World and Fashionable Advertiser* (15 May 1788).

11 *Morning Herald* (8 September 1788).

12 Henry Mayhew, *London Labour and the London Poor* (London, 1851), vol. 1, p. 177.

13 'Grand Rowing Match', *The Times* (1 February 1804).

14 *The Times* (20 May 1823).

15 'Advertisements and Notices', *Daily News* (13 April 1881).

16 Letter to the Editor, *The Times* (4 October 1882).

17 *New York American* (6 April 1898).

18 Joseph Pearson, *Pearson's Political Dictionary* (London, 1793), 's.SANDWICHES'.

19 *The Times* (6 February 1852).

20 *The Times* (20 July 1824; 21 December 1858).

21 Quoted in Alan Davidson, 'Le sandwich d'un joueur' in *Le Dossier: Casse-Croute: aliment portative, repas indéfinissale*, ed. Julia Csergo (Paris, 2001).

4 The American Sandwich

1 Eliza Leslie, *Directions for Cookery in its Various Branches*, (Philadelphia, 1840) p. 123.

2 Mrs T. J. Crowen, *Mrs Crowen's American Lady Cookery Book* (New York, 1866), pp. 329–30; Mrs. E. Putnam, *Mrs Putnam's Receipt Book and Young Housekeeper's Assistant* (New York, 1869), p. 110.

3 Marion H. Neil, *Salads, Sandwiches and Chafing Dish Recipes* (1916), pp. 91–2.

4 Jane and Michael Stern, *Roadfood Sandwiches* (New York, 2007), p. 3.

5 'Club Sandwich Rivals Hash', *Boston Daily Globe* (5 August 1900).

6 The Council of Jewish Women, *The Neighbourhood Cook*

Book (Portland OR, 1914), p. 282.

7 Florence A. Cowles, *Seven Hundred Sandwiches* (1928), p. 185.

8 *New York Times* (7 May 1930).

9 Richard J. S. Gutman, *The American Diner Then and Now* (Baltimore and London, 2000), p. 14.

10 Elizabeth McKeon and Linda Everett, *The American Diner Cookbook* (Nashville, TN, 2003), pp. 256–7.

11 Gutman, *American Diner*, p. 40.

12 Ibid., p. 97.

13 Jeff Guinn, *Go Down Together: The True, Untold Story of Bonnie and Clyde* (London and New York, 2009) p. 157.

14 Ibid., pp. 338–4.

15 Stern and Stern, *Roadfood Sandwiches*, p. 13.

16 R. W. Apple, 'In Hoagieland, They Accept No Substitutes', *New York Times* (28 May 2003).

17 William Robbins, 'About Philadelphia', *New York Times* (17 April 1984).

18 John F. Mariani, *The Encyclopedia of American Food and Drink* (New York, 1999), p. 154.

19 At www.loc.gov/rr/print/swann/blondie/food.html (accessed 25 November 2009).

20 Stern and Stern, *Roadfood Sandwiches*, p. 80.

5 The Global Sandwich

1 At http://chowhound.chow.com/topics/269669 (accessed November 2009).

2 Julia Moskin, 'Building on Layers of Tradition', *New York Times* (7 April 2009).

3 At www.banhmill.com; Bee Wilson, 'The Kitchen Thinker', *The Sunday Telegraph*, 18 April 2010.

4 *Oeuvres de Lord Byron*, trans. M. M. Amédée Pichot, vol. v (France 1830), translator's note.

5 Gwen Robyns, *The Book of Sandwiches* (London and Sydney, 1984), p. 14.

6 'Sandwich Courses', *The Economist* (5 February 2009).

7 At www.zenkimchi.com/FoodJournal/?p=1647 (accessed November 2009).

8 At http://forum.gaijinpot.com/showthread.php?t=71803 (accessed November 2009).

9 At www.davidappleyard.com/japan/jp9.htm (accessed November 2009).

10 Email to author (26 November 2009).

11 Carlye Adler, 'How China Eats a Sandwich', *Fortune Small Business* (1 March 2005).

12 Email to author (26 November 2009).

Select Bibliography

Abelson, Jenn, 'Arguments Spread Thick: Rivals Aren't Serving
    Same Food, Judge Rules', *The Boston Globe*, 10 November
    2006
Allen, M. L., *Five o' Clock Tea* (London, 1886)
Allen, Woody, *Getting Even* (New York, 1971)
Barnes, Donna R., and Peter G. Rose, *Matters of Taste: Food
    and Drink in Seventeeth-Century Dutch Art and Life* (Albany,
    NY, 2002)
Bevan, Judi, *The Rise and Fall of Marks and Spencer: And How it
    Rose Again* (London, 2007)
Bowen, Carol, *The Giant Sandwich Book* (London, 1981)
Boxer, Arabella, *Arabella Boxer's Book of English Food* (London,
    1993)
Brobeck, Florence, *The Lunch Box in Every Kind of Sandwich*
    (New York, 1946)
Bunyan, Nigel, 'Revealed: The Secrets of a British Rail
    Sandwich', *The Daily Telegraph*, 22 November 2002
Burton, David, *The Raj at Table* (London 1993)
Cadiou, Yvan, *Sandwiches and Then Some* (London, 2009)
Carter, Charles, *The Complete practical Cook, or, a new System of the
    Whole Art and Mystery of Cooking* (London, 1730)
Cowles, Florence A, *Five Hundred Sandwiches* (London, 1929)
—, *Seven Hundred Sandwiches* (Boston, 1929)
Crowen, Mrs T. J., *Mrs. Crowen's American Lady Cookery Book*
    (New York, 1866)

Davidson, Alan, 'Le sandwich d'un joueur', in *Le Dossier: Casse-Croute: aliment portative, repas indéfinissale*, ed. Julia Csergo (Paris, 2001)

Dodd, Philip B., *The Reverend Guppy's Aquarium:Encounters with the Heroes of the English Language* (London, 2007)

Dunnington, Rose, *Super Sandwiches: Wrap 'em Stack'em Stuff'em* (Asheville, NC, 2007)

Food Timeline, The, 'FAQs: sandwiches', www.foodtimeline.org/foodsandwiches.html

Fuller, Eva Greene,*The Up-to-Date Sandwich Book, 400 Ways to Make a Sandwich.* (Chicago, 1927)

Guinn, Jeff, *Go Down Together: The True, Untold Story of Bonnie and Clyde* (London and New York 2009)

Gutman, Richard J. S., *American Diner Then and Now* (Baltimore, 2000)

Hardy, Emma, *'Pret a Manger' Salads and Sandwiches, How to Make them At Home* (London, 1996)

Heath, Ambrose, *Good Sandwiches and Picnic Dishes* (London, 1948)

Herbert. T., *Salads and Sandwiches* (London, 1890)

Jack, Florence B., *One Hundred Salads and Sandwiches* (London, 1928)

Kirkpatrick, Catherine, *500 Recipes for Sandwiches and Packed Meals* (London, 1984)

Leslie, Eliza, *The Lady's Receipt-Book* (Philadelphia, PA, 1847)

Leyel, Mrs. C. F., *Cold Savoury Meals* (London,1927)

McKeon, Elizabeth, and Linda Everett, *The American Diner Cookbook* (Nashville, TN, 2003)

Mariani, John F. *The Encyclopedia of American Food and Drink* (New York, 1999)

Mason, Charlotte, *The Lady's assistant for regulating and supplying her table; containing one hundred and fifty select bills of fare* (London, 1773)

Mason, Laura, 'Everything Stops for Tea', in *Luncheon, Nuncheon and other Meals: Eating with the Victorians*, ed. C. Anne Wilson (London, 1994) pp. 71–91

Mayhew, Henry, *London Labour and London Poor* (London, 1851)

Mintel, *Sandwiches* (A Mintel Leisure Intelligence Report, Great Britain, 2001)

Miller, Stephen, *Starting and Running a Sandwich-Coffee Bar* (London, 2002)

Moran, Joe, *Queuing for Beginners: The Story of Daily Life from Breakfast to Bedtime* (London, 2007)

Morton, Mark, 'Bread and Meat for God's Sake', *Gastronomica* (Summer 2004), pp. 6–7

Neil, Marion Harris, *Salads, Sandwiches and Chafing Dish Recipes* (London, 1916)

Panati, Charles, *Panati's Extraordinary Origins of Everyday Things* (New York, 1987), p. 400

Parasher, U. D., L. Dow, R. L. Fankhauser et al., 'An Outbreak of Viral Gastroenteritis Associated with the Consumption of Sandwiches: Implications for the Control of Transmission by Food Handlers', *Epidemiology and Infection*, CXXI/3 (December 1998)

Pearson, Joseph, *Pearson's Political Dictionary* (London, 1793)

Peel, Cecilia, *Indian Curries, Soups and Sandwiches: A Complete Guide for European Housekeepers* (London 1931)

Putnam, Mrs E., *Mrs. Putnam's Receipt Book and Young Housekeeper's Assistant*, new and enlarged edition (New York, 1869)

Ray, John, *Observations Topographical, Moral and Physiological made in a Journey through part of the Low-Countries* (London, 1673)

Redington White, M., *Something New in Sandwiches* (London, 1933)

Renner, H. D., *The Origin of Food Habits* (London, 1944)

Rhodes, Hugh, *The Boke of Nurtur for Men Servants* (London, 1560)

Ridgway, Judy, *The Breville Toasted Sandwich Book* (Cambridge, 1982)

Robyns, Gwen, *The Book of Sandwiches* (London and Sydney, 1984)

Rodger, N.A.M., *The Insatiable Earl: A Life of John Montagu, Fourth Earl of Sandwich (1718–1792),* (London, 1993)

Rorer, S. T., *Sandwiches* (Philadelphia, PA, 1894)

Schama, Simon, *The Embarrassment of Riches* (London, 1987)

Shircliffe, Arnold, *The Edgewater Sandwich and Hors'd'oeuvre Book* (New York, 1975)

Sinclair, Rabbi Julian, 'Karich', *The Jewish Chronicle Online*, 21 August 2008

Smith, Andrew F., 'Sandwiches', entry in *The Oxford Encyclopedia of Food and Drink in America* (Oxford, 2004)

Southworth, May E., *One Hundred and One Sandwiches*, revd edn (San Francisco, CA, 1906)

Steele, Louise, *The Book of Sandwiches* (London and New York, 1989)

Stern, Jane and Stern, Michael, *Roadfood Sandwiches: Recipes and Lore from our Favourite Shops Coast to Coast* (New York, 2007)

Stuart, Tristram, *Waste: Uncovering the Global Food Scandal* (London, 2009)

Ward, Artemus *Sandwiches* (Montreal, 1870)

Weingarten, Susan, 'Haroset' in *Authenticity in the Kitchen: Proceedings on the Oxford Symposium on Food and Cookery 2005* (Totnes, 2006), pp. 414–27

Wilson, C. Anne, *Food and Drink in Britain: From the Stone Age to Recent Times* (London, 1973)

Woodman, Mary, *100 Varieties of Sandwiches and How to Prepare Them* (London, 1934)

Acknowledgements

I'd like to thank the following people, for help of various kinds: Sarah Ballard, Café Brazil (Cambridge), Ivan Day, Katherine Duncan-Jones, Janet Clarke, Svein Fossa, Gonzalo Gil, Deborah Hamilton, Lara Heimert, Spencer Hooks, Martha Jay, Paul Keller, Michael Leaman, Anne Malcolm, Orlando Montagu, Rosie Nicholls/ Luchford APM, Gaitri Pagrach-Chandra, Judith Pagrach, Elfreda Pownall, Miri Rubin, Cathy Runciman, David Runciman, Natasha Runciman, Tom Runciman, Helen Saberi, Andrew F. Smith, Dan Silverston of the Soho Sandwich Co., Ray Sokolov, Nate Steiner, Tristram Stuart, Andrew Wilson and Emily Wilson.

Photo Acknowledgements

Photo © adlifemarketing/2010 iStock International Inc.: p. 86; photos author: pp. 12, 23, 29, 42, 43, 51, 57, 89, 95, 99, 102; British Museum, London (photo © Trustees of the British Museum): p. 20; courtesy of Janet Clarke/Peter Brears: p. 39; photo © creacart/2010 iStock International Inc.: p. 37; photo © Culinary Archives & Museum, Providence, RI: p. 45; photo Daily Mail/Rex Features: p. 55; photo Dick Doughty/*Saudi Aramco World*/SAWDIA: p. 91; photo © FA/Roger-Viollet: p. 56; courtesy of George Eastman House, International Museum of Photography and Film (© Nickolas Muray Photo Archives): p. 81; Getty Images: p. 34; image courtesy of Deborah Hamilton: p. 71; photo Spencer Hooks: p. 85; photo reproduced by permission of Paul Keller: p. 104; by permission of The Lanesborough Hotel, London: p. 63; photo Michael Leaman/Reaktion Books: p. 47; Library of Congress, Washington, DC: p. 65; photo David McEnery/Rex Features: p. 58; photo Robyn Mackenzie/BigStockPhoto: p. 28; photo Mattes: p. 106; photo monkeybusinessimages/BigStockPhoto: p. 13; photo Nickolas Muray, by kind permission of Mimi Muray Leavitt: p. 81; National Archive of the Netherlands: p. 67; National Maritime Museum, London (Greenwich Hospital Collection): p. 17; private collection: p. 78; Robert Opie collection: pp. 38, 70; photo Roger-Viollet/Rex Features: p. 72; reproduced courtesy of Dan Silverston/The Soho Sandwich company: p. 8; photo © sixty7a/2010 iStock International Inc.: p. 59; photo Sky Picture Group/Rex Features: p. 107; Ron Spillman/Rex Features: p. 11; image courtesy of Nate Steiner: p. 27; photo stock.xchng: p. 9; Szathmary Family Culinary Collection: p. 45; Time & Life Pictures/Getty Images: p. 18; photo TS/Keystone USA/Rex Features: p. 66; photo Daniel Young: p. 93.

Index

italic numbers refer to illustrations; **bold** to recipes

148